Vanishing Ireland

Further Chronicles of a Disappearing World

VANISHING IRELAND

Further Chronicles of a Disappearing World

JAMES FENNELL AND TURTLE BUNBURY

HACHETTE
BOOKS
IRELAND

To William Fennell (1941–2008),
a man of inestimable kindness, intelligence and support.

To our youngest daughters,
Mimi Fennell and Bay Bunbury.

Copyright © 2009 photographs, James Fennell
Copyright © 2009 text, Turtle Bunbury

First published in 2009 by Hachette Books Ireland
An Hachette UK Company

3

The right of James Fennell and Turtle Bunbury to be identified as the Authors of the Work has been asserted by them
in accordance with the Copyright, Designs and Patents Act, 1988.

A CIP catalogue record for this title is available from the British Library.

'Shanagolden' by Sean McCarthy

ISBN 978 0340 92027 5

Typeset in Garamond by Anú Design, Tara
Cover and text design by Anú Design, Tara
Printed and bound in Great Britain by Butler Tanner & Dennis, Frome

Hachette Books Ireland policy is to use papers that are natural, renewable and recyclable products and made from
wood grown in sustainable forests. The logging and manufacturing processes are expected to conform to the
environmental regulations of the country of origin.

Hachette Books Ireland
8 Castlecourt Centre
Castleknock
Dublin 15
Ireland

A division of Hachette UK, 338 Euston Road, London NW1 3BH, England

CONTENTS

INTRODUCTION

Not so long ago, I rambled into one of Eddie McDonald's monthly music nights in Clonmore, County Carlow. About sixty senior citizens from the surrounding area were crammed on wooden benches inside Eddie's barn. They were there to entertain and to be entertained. Most sang songs, some humorous and rowdy, others unspeakably sad. A skinny labourer whistled a tune called 'Bird Song'. A ruddy cheeked cattle farmer simply danced to the sound of all those ancient feet tapping in a circle around him. A ninety-four-year-old woman played on a fiddle she had inherited from her Scottish grandfather. When I commended her later, she nudged my shoulder and said, 'Sure it's not all hip-hop, hey?'

It was an epic and courageous night. During one particularly beautiful song, I watched as many of those gathered in the barn closed their eyes and rewound their memories to younger days of stray kisses and near misses and harvest moons where raindrops fell on muddy boots and red lips curled upwards in contagious smiles that grew wider and deeper and older and wiser and wetter and sadder as the scattered memories of collective youth swooped through the barn.

The people gathered in Clonmore that night were of the same generation that we have recorded in these pages. Almost all were born before the Second World War. The oldest person in this book, Statia Kealy, was born in 1903. Her mother was born in 1862, before the bicycle was invented. Statia was one of thirteen children, although six of her siblings died in childhood. Many Irish mothers gave birth to a dozen or more children in those times. The McFaddens of Ballymote, County Sligo, have a tradition of producing twelve children every generation.

For most of the twentieth century, Irish children walked to school. Many went barefoot, although Jim O'Malley says he wore shoes in the winter. Baby Rudden of County Cavan recalls how her father would walk ahead of her and her siblings, to sweep back the thistles and 'beat the water off the ferns on the rocks so we'd not get our legs wet'.

Schools were rudimentary places. In Eugene Brady's school in Abbeylara, County Longford, every child had to bring their own turf for the fire. Not that the heat would ever reach you, says Mick King. His teacher always kept his posterior firmly by the fireplace and took all the heat for himself.

Johnny Golden is one of the few people in this volume who treasured his schooldays, which he spent at the Sunbeam Orphanage in Bray, County Wicklow. Most of the other characters interviewed in this book were slapped, smacked or otherwise assaulted at school. Teachers come across as a universally despised and feared race. But that is the way people were in those times, points out Frank O'Brien of Athy, County Kildare. Sligo farmer Joe Muldoon was less philosophical when he met his old teacher some years after he left school; he couldn't stop himself from letting loose with his fists.

Many left school before they were fourteen to help out at home. Statia Kealy's earliest memories involve coming straight home from school to help cut turf and pick potatoes. Sister Alphonsus was similarly occupied from an early age at her family's farm in County Limerick. She says farming was a much more sociable way of life back then, before the tractors came along. From the age of nine, Bart Nolan rose at five in the morning and made his way down to Dublin's fruit and vegetable markets to see if he could make some extra money.

For some, the workplace offered a chance of further education. Betty Scott of County Carlow was taught how to read and write by the lady of the Big House where she went to work at the age of fifteen. Edward Hayes was taught how to drive by a Protestant clergyman and mastered the social graces when, as a young stable boy, he was drafted in to help serve dinner in the houses of the Kilkenny gentry.

For others, the real education was to be found at home. Mary Maddison honed her immense story-telling skills by listening to the melodic tales and sean nós of her uncles, fishermen on the islands of West Cork. Frank O'Brien learned more than he ever needed to know about life on the Western Front from the shell-shocked soldiers who assembled in his father's bar when the pensions came in. Jim Kielty heard similar tales driving his taxi around County Sligo in the 1930s. Bernie Dwyer was taught history by his grandmother, whose parents had lived through the cholera epidemic that crippled Sligo in the 1830s.

The middle decades of the twentieth century were difficult ones for Ireland. With a stagnant economy, emigration was often the only option. James McGarvey of Clones, County Monaghan, left to build the railroads of Britain at the age of fourteen and stayed thirty years. P.J. Davis of Ennistymon, County Clare, similarly spent a quarter of a century working in car factories and steelworks in England. Limerick farmer Jack Connolly joked that 'only the fool stayed behind' after all his brothers and uncles left Ireland. Francie McFadden muscled up as a labourer in London, but his neighbour, Willie Davey, found it harder to secure a job and returned to Sligo a few years later. Both Mick King of County Mayo and Nellie Kelly of Nenagh, County Tipperary, were preparing to settle in London when a call for help from the home-land brought them back. Neither left Ireland again.

Some people have nomadic genes. It is well over 200 years since John Carson's family stayed in the same place for more than two generations. But for others, like Jim 'Tailor' O'Malley and Mick King, the land they till is the same their ancestors worked on hundreds of years ago. Farming is not an easy slog. Denny Galvin gave up when the public road that cut through his farm in north Kerry became too busy to herd his cattle.

Denny Galvin, Jim Tailor and Mick King are all bachelor farmers. That is unexceptional for twentieth-century rural Ireland and there are many like them in this book. One said he had loved many women, but never enough to change their name. Kerry brothers Stevie and Timmy Kelleher are delighted they never got wed as it has enabled them to a life of independence. At the age of 106, Statia Kealy hasn't ruled out finding a husband yet. She says there was a man once, but the drink got the better of him.

Betty Scott and the Kelleher brothers were all born of arranged marriages. But love was in the air for many in that generation. Mary Maddison met her late husband working on an Atlantic cruise ship. Billy and Cathy Dowling met at one of the house dances which were once so popular in the Irish countryside. Mick Lavelle met his late wife in the kitchen of Newport House when he was a porter and she was a cook. Liam and Maureen O'Shea have just celebrated their golden wedding anniversary, while Frank and Tríona O'Brien are closing in on fifty-eight years together.

While the economic boom time of the Celtic Tiger was undoubtedly good for Irish confidence, many older people have been unsettled by the speed with which the younger generations have been willing to abandon the past. The pace of life has changed utterly, along with our expectations and priorities. The elders regard the last century as a happier, gentler age. Liam O'Shea reckons the car has a lot to answer for. Before the car, everyone who passed by his father's Kerry forge would call in for a cup of tea and a chat. Now everyone speeds by with perhaps a curt wave or a honk of the horn.

There is also a belligerent undercurrent in our society that remains unchecked. Eileen Hall feels it when the souped-up boy racers howl past her small rural shop in County Monaghan. The senior citizens of Ballymote feel it on the streets of their small town on Friday nights. Stevie Kelleher of Kerry is appalled by the emergence of gangs in the cities and bigger towns. Joan Crowley says Kenmare is still a peaceful town but even the streets around her pub can get unbearably noisy by night.

We have become a stay-at-home people and we rarely interact with our neighbours. For the older generation, this poses a considerable dilemma as immobility and loneliness creep in. The friendly villages of their youth are an increasing rarity, either because the post office or pub (and almost certainly the creamery) have closed down, or because the fields around them have been developed into anonymous housing estates and retail parks. Most Irish farms are now framed by tarmac roads, supporting a relentless convoy of whizzing cars, lorries and motorbikes. Such roads are no place for the black High Nellie bikes of our grandparents' generation. Mind you, if you're on the roads of County Leitrim, watch out for Johnny Golden purring by on his Honda 70. And his neighbour, the forester Johnny Fyfe, might yet clamber up on his old BSA 150. But for Francie McFadden and Jim O'Malley, the safest way to travel is on a tractor.

The concept of the 'Vanishing Ireland' project is simply to chronicle a cross section of Irish society that is slowly fading from our world. The feedback we received for the first volume of *Vanishing Ireland* was both astonishing and deeply encouraging. Many letters came from people who wished they had taken the time to write down the stories of their now deceased family elders. For this volume, as with the first, we have sought out souls of a positive nature who do not simply link us to the past but, perhaps more importantly, provide us with wisdom and humour to take on the future.

James and I hope this second volume continues the interest started by the first. It has been an immense privilege for us to listen to these stories, to have the past reincarnated by those who lived through it. We do not intend to cease recording such aspects of Irish life until we ourselves vanish.

Turtle Bunbury, July 2009

OF CATTLE, FISH,

PUMPKINS AND TREES

BABY RUDDEN

Born 1923

Farmer

Drumcor, Redhills, County Cavan

'Well? What do you think of this country?' asks Baby Rudden, chucking some turf into the Smith and Wellstead stove. Baby has not travelled a great deal in her life. In fact, the farthest she got 'was to the cattle byre at the back of the shed, and maybe out in the hayfield the odd time'. 'It's hard to escape with all the animals,' she explains – although, in truth, she did make a few 'long journeys' to Dublin in 2006 when her late brother, John, was taken ill.

The country to which Baby refers is a silent labyrinth of grassy hills, winding lakes and lonely trees, two miles east of the Cavan village of Redhills. She has farmed this land all her life and now lives alone. The remoteness of the farmstead is made all the more poignant when she explains that, in her childhood, the area was replete with forty or more stone cottages and the laughter of children. 'They're all dead and gone out of the houses now,' she says.

Most of the cottages she knew have vanished into this difficult, scratchy earth, but there are still some scattered about, though their grey, wet, crumbling walls are inching ever downwards.

One of the few houses still operating is the farm where her father, Benny Rudden, was born, which stands just across the valley in Callowhill, where the Ruddens have been living since at least the 1840s. The house was thatched in Baby's youth but has been modernised by relatives in recent times.

In the spring of 1921, Benny Rudden inherited the farm at Drumcor and built the cottage in which his daughter now lives. He made it with 'sand, stones and materials he dug from the land here'. Ireland was a rapidly changing country. The Big House at Redhills, owned by the White-Venables, was burned to the ground that summer. By the end of the year, a new political border had been created between the Irish Free State and Northern Ireland, less than three miles from the Rudden farmstead.

Within a few years of moving to Drumcor, Benny was a married man. Born in the house in 1923, Bridget – or Baby – was the eldest of his four children. Her only sister, Alice, was born in 1925 but succumbed to meningitis when she was nineteen, just weeks after her wedding. Meningitis also killed Baby's brother, Little Matt, in 1946, when he was just seventeen. That left Baby and her youngest brother, John, who was born in 1931. 'He was the pet,' she says.

Along with a portrait of Jesus, photographs of Baby's family adorn the walls of her kitchen, scattered between the stove and a dresser filled with dusty plates and cups. She shares the room with two dogs: Darst, a faithful old timer who used to ride up on the tractor with her brother John, and Spot, a lively youngster inherited from a neighbour. When it comes to business, Baby is canniness personified and you simply will not pull the wool over this woman's eyes. Her farm is all about animals. In the past two years, she has tarred the dirt track avenue and replaced a series of old corrugated huts with a handsome 14,000-square-foot shed, which houses her thirty-strong herd of beefy, muscular cattle and healthy sucklers, with golden-red Limousin and docile Herefords in the ascendance. Baby knows each cow and takes time to bottle feed an orphaned calf during our tour. The shed makes life much easier for her, but she finds the doors hard to close. 'I need to eat more Weetabix,' she laughs.

The cattle have plenty of company. Adjacent to Baby's house is a small line of scraggly damson trees, where two peaceable she-goats munch grass. Three muddy ducks, two drakes, a goose, a proud rooster and a seemingly tame flock of pigeons promenade alongside the whitewashed walls. Her guinea fowl were lately decimated by a wicked fox, but her chickens are securely compounded between an oil tanker and two dilapidated vehicles – a VW Caravelle and a Renault Trafic – set upon a grassy knoll above the house. A legacy of her late brother is the rear lights stapled to the trees. He used to hang empty Castrol GTX cans along a clothesline between the trees and, when asked the purpose of the display, replied, 'Every man should have something that no other man has.'

To get to school in Killoughter, the young Ruddens made their barefooted way across fields and bogs on a journey that 'would take near an hour'. In wet weather, their father sometimes walked with them. 'He used to beat the water off the ferns on the rocks so we'd not get our legs wet.' There was a good roaring fire at school to dry off. 'We had to gather whins [gorse] off the rocks to get the fire going.' The teacher was a rough drunkard, seemingly inclined to cure his whiskey hangover by welting children across the bottom with a knotty blackthorn stick.

Baby Rudden left school at the age of twelve and went to help her parents. She never married but, instead, devoted her life to the farm. Her parents died 'in the one year' in the 1970s. She and John ran the farm after that, without fuss or complication. One of the most exciting events of the 1990s was when Hollywood came to Redhills to film not one but two movies – *The Playboys* and *The Run of the Country*. Local lads, employed as extras, were frequently seen glugging whiskey from the neck of a bottle and then hiding the bottles behind their backs the moment the wives showed up.

In a previous generation, Baby Rudden is the sort of woman who would have smoked a pipe. She speaks with a strong accent that softens with familiarity and though she has lived through considerable hardships, she retains a wonderful warmth encapsulated in her shy smile. She likes to read and watches the news on television. She does not believe in ghosts, but has a keen interest in the goings on of everyone in the parish and is intrigued by the particular burial arrangements for the recently departed. She loves having people over to visit, to sit around on chairs and talk the talk, before heading on home when time suits. A few nights earlier, Baby hosted a spontaneous gathering for 'six or seven' local friends in her kitchen. Such occasions are increasingly rare, she says. 'There's nobody wants anyone in the house now. They won't let you in!'

DENIS GALVIN

Born 1945

Cattle Farmer

Stradbally, County Kerry

Denny Galvin is standing precisely where we were told he would be – leaning against a wall, beside the telephone box, watching the autumnal traffic whizz through the small village of Stradbally. Over and above his 'big, long fleece of a beard', his brooding eyes latch on to us as we approach and he holds a level gaze.

'Are you Denny?'

'I'd say so.'

'How're you doing?'

'Well, there'd be no use my complaining to anyone because they won't listen.'

'Are you not feeling well?'

'No,' says Denny. 'But I'm pleased to meet you anyway. What townland do you come from?'

Denny is his father's only son. He was born at the tail end of the Second World War on a small 'kind of a farm' here on the northern side of the Dingle peninsula. His childhood was spent helping out with a herd of dairy cattle, often driving the pony and cart down to the creamery in Stradbally with the milk. 'But then the old fellow died and so, next thing, sell out!' He says the last two words loudly and triumphantly.

For twenty years, Denny attempted to run the farm but, eventually, the odds got the better of him. Today, he leases the forty-six acres and spends his days standing by the wall.

'I had several different occupations in the farming line,' he explains. 'And any one of them wouldn't work because farms around here are too small.'

Denny replaced his father's dairy herd with sucklers, eighteen cows and a bull, bringing the calves to the markets of Castleisland and Listowel. Everything was running relatively smoothly until the farm was hit by an outbreak of tuberculosis. Denny was instructed to destroy his herd, save for two cows and the bull. 'What do I want two cows and a bull for?' he asks. 'The bull was going mad around the field with two little cows.' And so, the two cows and the bull were sold. Denny had a crack at dry cattle 'until everything got too dear and I sold them and then I let the land'.

Denny says the trouble with the farm was that it was too scattered. 'There's a piece of it here down the road. There's a part of it on the strand. And there's a part of it away up the high road. That's the way of many of the farms around here.' In Denny's father's day, this wasn't a problem because there wasn't much traffic on the road, but today, with so many cars and buses constantly driving past, it would be very difficult to herd cattle from one field to another.

Denny's home is a short walk from the village, up a laneway 'beside the bushes'. He says he is content to live on his own and watch the world go by. He has three sisters, married and living elsewhere in the county who call in from time to time. He also receives regular visits from the postman who, all too often, bears brown envelopes, which Denny calls 'the window ones'. 'That's all that's come lately is bills,' he says. 'And the best time for them is coming on to Christmas. That's when they all turn up.'

When Denny is thirsty, he would be inclined to head down the road to Castlegregory. 'But I don't like walking,' he confesses.

Denny has a tendency to speak in riddles. When asked his age, he replies with a gentle cuss, 'Stop a minute, if I were hung by a rope since I was in my early fifties, I'd be pretty quare looking by now.'

We have just managed to work out the year of his birth when a car turns up his lane, sending Denny's head into a 360-degree spin. 'I must be chasing him,' he says, getting to his feet. 'See you another time.' And off he trots off into the bushes.

EUGENE BRADY

Born 1931

Farmer

Camagh, Abbeylara, County Longford

'It was him who started it,' says Eugene, pointing to his son, James. 'I'd never even seen a pumpkin before. A turnip I had seen in my young days, but never a pumpkin.' James is about to get into his car and return to Dublin where he works as a landscape gardener. His father stalls his departure. '1995 was the year Kerry won the All-Ireland,' he continues, 'but it was also the year myself and James won the Pumpkin of the Year. And I tell you, there was more carry on about that pumpkin than there was over Kerry winning the Sam Maguire.'

When Eugene recalls that first sweet victory, his entire face crumples into a huge, contagious grin. It's hard to believe this sprightly farmer is knocking on eighty years old. The speed of his nod-wink greeting is particularly impressive. Even though he is recovering from a rare dose of the flu, his speech is rapid, fluent and peppered with humour. It's almost impossible to get a word in. When emphasising a point, his eyes latch on to mine and his entire chin tilts into his breastplate.

Eugene was the second of eight children born into a farming family outside Granard, County Longford. His father, James, was a popular man, much admired for his brute strength during the annual tug of war championships. 'My old fellow was one of the strongest men in Ireland,' maintains Eugene. 'Holy Jayzus, the big shoulders on him.'

From the farm, young Eugene and his siblings walked to school in Abbeylara – passing by the eerie ruins of the Cistercian abbey en route – carrying their own turf for the school fire. Eugene left school shortly before his fourteenth birthday and 'landed back' at home to help out on the farm. He earned two shillings a day picking spuds for the neighbours. I expect this busy soul was able to pick a fierce amount of spuds when he was a teenager.

At the age of eighteen, Eugene secured a job with Bord na Móna, the state-owned turf company, which was then in its infancy. He was based in the company's factory at Abbeyshrule and would work there for the next thirty-five years, travelling to work on a bicycle because 'nobody had a car back then and boy racers went about on their feet'. In the early days there was no tap at Abbeyshrule so, much as he carried his own turf to school, he brought his own water to work.

In 1975, Eugene was appointed supervisor and given charge of fifty employees. 'That means I'd be telling you what to do instead of you telling me,' he says. In truth, his brief was considerable as it was during this time that Bord na Móna upgraded its mechanised harvesting techniques along the extensive boglands of Longford, Westmeath and Offaly. Up until this point, most people had used raw peat sods for their fires but Bord na Móna was now offering briquettes of shredded peat, compressed into a virtually smokeless, slow-burning fuel that was easy to carry and easy to store. The company was also supplying peat to all the Electricity Supply Board's power stations.

On a more personal level, Eugene was involved with the development of peat moss, a combination of peat and soil, which became popular with gardeners, particularly those with potted plants and greenhouses. Perhaps it was Eugene's intrinsic understanding of the power of peat that propelled the pumpkins of Camagh to victory in the 1995 National Pumpkin Championships. Certainly, his wheelbarrow has carted a good deal of nutritious dark-brown soil down to the greenhouse where his pumpkins grow. Beside the greenhouse lie eighteen drills of potatoes and vegetables, all for home consumption. But it is within the polytunnel itself that the real beauties are born. Jack o' Lanterns. Autumn Golds. Connecticut Fields. Atlantic Giants – the present favourite for pumpkin contests. Eugene treats each pumpkin with a sharp, competitive eye. A founding father of the Virginia Pumpkin Festival in County Cavan, he is a regular exhibitor across Ireland. In 2005 and 2006, he had back-to-back victories in the National Championships, latterly with a whopper weighing twenty-five stones.

Today Eugene grows up to 500 pumpkins a year, primarily for the Hallowe'en market, to rest on gateposts and side-tables with candles burning brightly within. Others are destined for pumpkin soup, some are sold to Fyffes and any remaining stock is chucked into the cattle feed. Eugene says the crop is entirely weather dependent and some years are utterly hopeless.

The Brady farm, which Eugene bought in 1961, occupies some of the drier land in this boggy neighbourhood. On still nights, you can hear the brown waters of the River Inny, which forms the border between Westmeath and Longford, flowing beneath the nearby Camagh Bridge. While Eugene's younger son, James, and two daughters live elsewhere in Ireland, his eldest son, John, now runs the farm, looking after the forty-five cattle and a second, smaller farm at Granard.

There is no doubt, however, that Eugene's most peaceful moments are to be found when he is tending his pumpkins, oblivious to the sound of barking dogs and boy racers motoring down those long, infinite bog roads.

JIM 'TAILOR' O'MALLEY

Born August 1925

Farmer

Kilsallagh, County Mayo

Jim O'Malley's eyes traverse the skyline from the Sheeffrey Hills to majestic Mweelrea rising beyond. 'There wasn't any place around that I didn't walk,' he says. 'I hunted all over those hills. Fowling mostly. Me and the dog, looking for partridge and grouse. But I'm a little too old for that craic now.'

You wouldn't think it. Perhaps it's the damp Mayo air but this fresh-faced bachelor does not look eighty-four.

He lives on a windswept shoulder of Croagh Patrick, just above the Atlantic. Through the window panes of his kitchen, you can see the dark rolling waters of the ocean and the blue glow of Inishturk Island. On the hill beside the house are the shadowy remains of other cottages that stood before the Famine.

'This house is here about two and a half hundred years,' says Jim. The farm belonged to his mother's people, the O'Grádaighs. It is a small farm of seventeen acres, split into a handful of fields. Standing at the top of his property, you can see the strip quite clearly. Its borders were delineated by the Land Commission, which acquired the freehold on this coastline from Lord Sligo in the 1880s. Jeremiah, a shy and aged donkey, lives in the closest field. On other slopes, in other people's fields, you can see the heads of other donkeys and ponies jutting above the rocky walls and khaki grasses.

The O'Grádaigh women lived as long as trees. Jim's mother was 102 when she passed away in 1984. Her mother lived to be ninety-eight, and her grandmother lived to over 100 – the latter was a small child when General Humbert's doomed French army captured Westport in 1798.

In about 1880, Jim's grandfather, Martin O'Grádaigh, married a midwife who Jim knew only as 'An Oneen', meaning 'a small old woman'. Every morning, as they left for school, Jim would light her clay pipe. 'First, you'd get a tráithnín [a rush] and clean the pipe. Then you'd get a bit of straw and twist it into a little sugán [platted straw]. You'd put the yoke into the fire and when it was lit, you'd light the pipe.'

'My father was a tailor,' he explains, 'and I go by the name of Jim Tailor because there are so many O'Malleys here.' This is, indeed, O'Malley country and has been at least since Grace O'Malley, the Pirate Queen, ruled the Mayo coastline 500 years ago. 'Even to this day, they talk about her,' he marvels.

James O'Malley, the tailor, secured the O'Grádaigh farm when he married Martin O'Grádaigh's daughter in 1915. He was a tall man, with a twirling, handlebar moustache, eleven years senior to his wife. 'But,' says Jim with one eyebrow arched, 'they had nine in the family, so he wasn't bad at it.' His tailoring business was chiefly suits and trousers, but there was plenty of trade making báinín, white woollen jackets, the wool for which was sent up from a sheep farmer in the bogs of Mullagh.

Born in this house in 1925, Jim was the seventh of the nine children. All his siblings married and most settled in England. All are gone now, save for a younger sister living in London. Many of his aunts and uncles emigrated to Chicago in the early twentieth century and Jim frequently plays host to distant cousins from the New World. 'Oh, cripes, they come regular to me,' he laughs. Not all the O'Grádaighs fared well in America. His uncle, Patrick Grady, was drinking in a tavern in Chicago when a drunkard 'shot him through the hole of the key in the door'. When Jim visited Chicago, he called on Patrick's grave and was delighted to see 'Kilsallagh' engraved on the headstone.

Jim was educated at the school in Kilsallagh, 'a half hour walk on our feet'. They had shoes in winter but, once May Day came, the shoes were gone. He disliked his teacher, who he recalls as a power-happy bully with a stick. 'At that time, the teacher, the priest and the garda had all the power,' he says. 'And they were all in it together.' Despite this, he is still loyal to the Catholic Church and a regular attendee at Lecanvey. 'I wouldn't turn my back on the Church,' he says. 'And I'm a real Fianna Fáil man, too. I'll support any man that's in Fianna Fáil, no matter what they done. I voted Fianna Fáil all my life and will do until I die.' There's a cryptic twinkle in his eyes.

When they were young, the O'Malley family walked everywhere, or travelled by pony and trap. In later years, there was a black High Nellie bike but it was tricky pedalling around the sandy roads before they became 'blacktops', as Jim refers to the tarmac. Jim never learned to drive. 'I tried once but I got nervous,' he says. 'I was headed for the ditches.' Since he gave up the bike, kindly neighbours have escorted him around and chauffeured him to the pub.

James O'Malley taught his children how to swim, a useful skill for coastal dwellers. 'In their generation, they were great swimmers,' says Jim. 'My father could swim three miles out to sea.' Being so close to the ocean, seafood was a regular part of the family diet. The young O'Malleys frequently combed the rocks of Clew Bay when the tide was out. They'd return with sweet-cans crammed with periwinkles (weevon), mussels (baghnach), crannach and slouk. Jim still keeps a bag of an edible red seaweed called dillisk in his fridge. He maintains that boiled dillisk can be 'as good as steak'. Up until recent years, he often ventured out in a fishing boat with his cousin, looking for 'mackerel and cold fish' in the waters around Clare Island and Inishturk. It is clear that Jim was not just a keen hunter and fisherman but also a fine cook. He keeps a near-spotless kitchen and bakes his own bread in the gas oven.

Jim left school at fourteen and began working for a family near Louisburg, gardening, milking the cow and taking the children out on a trap. By the age of twenty, he was cutting turf on the Bog of Allen in County Kildare, where he stayed 'for the weight of three years'. In the pubs of Kildare, the barmen would leave 'big white enamel jugs' of porter on the table and everyone would help themselves. 'The black cow's milk, we called it,' says Jim. He later went to work for an old farmer near Newbridge, milking thirty-five cows daily by hand and then carting the milk to the creamery.

When his father died in 1958, Jim took on the farm. Despite his adopted name, he wasn't tempted to take on the tailoring business. 'I couldn't thread a needle,' he confesses. A sheltered courtyard behind his house leads out through whitewashed sheds to the barn and fields beyond. A pile of turf in one shed exudes the promise of warmth. A paddle of ducks, including a marvellous Indian Runner, waddle round and round a sycamore tree by the barn. A mink has lately savaged some of his chickens but Jim is hopeful that his trusty hound, Sam, will beat the mink away when next it strikes. Otherwise, this is a quiet little farm.

Jim was never married, or tempted to marry, but knew a lot of women in his time. 'A lot of women,' he repeats wistfully. That said, he is still recovering from seeing a Mormon gentleman on the *Late Late Show* who had seven wives. 'Ah now, sure, the wives were lovely,' he granted. 'But they must be gone upstairs to be taking with a man like that.'

Jim is a regular down in Staunton's of Lecanvey, one of the finest old-school pubs in these parts, where they have musical evenings every Sunday. Jim's party piece is 'Shanagolden', which he sings with such a strong quiver that you can feel the chill from Croagh Patrick when he hits the high notes:

> *The cold winds from the mountains are calling soft to me,*
> *The smell of scented heather brings bitter memories,*
> *The wild and lonely eagle, up in the summer sky,*
> *Flies high on Shanagolden, where my young Willy lies.*

'Sure anyone can sing,' he says. 'People just don't know they can.'

GEORGE THOMAS

1926–2009

Farmer

Greenane Mor, County Wicklow

In the spring of 2008, George Thomas accepted that a chapter of his life had come to an end and closed the door of the mountain farmstead where he had lived for nearly seventy of his eighty-three years. George was, without doubt, one of the last of his kind. He lived without electricity or mechanisation. He had no car and saw no need for an avenue. His one-storey farmhouse was hidden in a field behind a hedge of cypress trees near sunny Greenane Mor. To access the property, you had to open a red gate from the road and walk across a grassy meadow – sheep on one side, heather on the other, with the glacial slopes of Glenmalure rising in the distance. Two strips of box hedge and a rickety gate pointed straight to his front door. In former times, the baker left a loaf of bread by the red gate. The postman left his mail there too.

The ambience of George's home was unquestionably serene. We have already become too accustomed to the persistent buzz and crackle of electrical goods. In George's paraffin-lit kitchen, the only sound was the turf burning on the vast open hearth, the fire gently fanned by a wheel-operated, under-floor pipe. Above the fire was the crane with a couple of hanging pots, used by George for both baking and cooking. The pots and kettle could be raised, lowered or moved sideways as the occasion demanded. The décor was simple and rustic, a photograph of de Valera and a poster of a cannabis plant hung mischievously between a sheet detailing upcoming events at the Rathdrum Historical Society which he used to frequent.

George loved to talk of bygone times. Charles Stewart Parnell, who lived in nearby Avondale, was one of his heroes. So, too, was de Valera. Many who frequent pubs such as M.J. Byrne's of Greenane or The Cartoon Inn of Rathdrum have benefited from George's wise words and historical anecdotes, delivered while he drank bottled Guinness served at room temperature.

George traced his father's side to the prosperous Rhondda Valley in Wales. They came to Ireland with Cromwell and were rewarded with land in County Wexford. By 1900, his grandfather, John Loftus Thomas, was farming sixty acres at Sheephouse, County Wexford, where he lived with his wife, Lucy, and their seven children.

In May 1910, tragedy struck when fifty-year-old Lucy was drowned. *The Irish Times* explained that she had become 'strange in her manner of late' to such an extent that her daughter, Eva, was about to inform

the family rector of her condition. When Lucy did not return from an egg-collecting venture one morning, her twenty-four-year-old son, Alfred, set off to find her. He discovered her body at the bottom of a marl hole.

Soon after Lucy's death, John Loftus Thomas took his three sons to Australia. By 1913, he had returned to Ireland and bought the farm at Greenane Mor. The eighteenth-century house once belonged to the Grant family, close allies of the rebel patriot Michael Dwyer who had a safe-house nearby.

In 1924, Alfred married Sarah Williams in a church near Greenane. Like the Thomases, the Williamses were of Welsh origin. During the eighteenth century, they ran a blacksmith's forge near the Vale of Clara. In the aftermath of the 1798 Rising, it was noted that the Williams family, although Protestant, had been involved in the manufacture of pikes for the rebel army. Perhaps this explains why Sarah's grandparents were evicted from their home in the 1850s. 'They were left on the side of the road, with a big family of children,' said George. 'It was most unusual for Protestants to be evicted like that. They were taken in by the Brady family of Ballinderry Cross. Wasn't that a very charitable act, for a Catholic family to do that for a Protestant family?'

As Sarah's mother had died when she was young, she was raised by her father, Paddy Williams, a sheep-farmer who kept his flock on the slopes of Ballinacor. 'Paddy never went to school and he couldn't read or write,' said George. 'But he could sing a powerful song and, with his long flowing beard, was a legend far and wide.'

Alfred and Sarah had two children, Eileen, born in 1925, and George, born in 1926. In April 1930, Alfred moved the family to South Dublin, where he found work as a gardener in Terenure. The Terenure of George's childhood was a landscape of flourishing gardens, small estates and empty roads where children played. He collected cigarette cards, treasuring each footballer, ship, horse and film star he acquired. 'My dad only smoked a pipe so that was my handicap, but I had no qualms about approaching strangers who were smoking and asking, "Have you any cigarette cards?" You wouldn't do that now!'

George's grandfather died in 1937 and, three years later, his father, Alfred, moved the family from Terenure to Greenane and took on the farm. Alfred's sister, Elsie, also lived with them during these years. When not working on the farm, George's teenage years were spent cycling to race meetings in Punchestown and the Point-to-Point's in Ballyknockan with his friend, the late Tommy Snell.

In 1952, his sister emigrated to Australia, where she still lives today. Sarah accompanied her to London from where she caught the boat. Devastated by her departure, Alfred, a non-drinker, went to the pub to drown his sorrows. He continued to run the farm until his death in 1966 aged eighty-two, when George took the helm. George's mother, Sarah, passed away in 1974 and Aunt Elsie in 1977.

George conceded that he would never have been allowed to live his old-world existence if he had married. 'You couldn't bring any lady to live under my conditions,' he said. 'It's been declared unfit for human habitation – but luckily I'm not human.' It was to be tricky for him to bring a girlfriend home to the family farm when his parents lived there. And after they died, he had to look after his aunt, whom he adored. By the time she died, George was fifty-one years old and ready to enjoy his bachelorhood.

George knew that his days in the antiquated homestead were numbered. His last hen died the week before we visited and he felt the death marked the end of an era. He was also somewhat blessed when, riddled with pneumonia and pleurisy, he was found unconscious in his bed by an Australian relative who happened to be staying with him that night. It was not often that George Thomas had guests to stay. Until his decease in June 2009, George was one of the cheeriest residents of St Colman's Hospital, Rathdrum. At his funeral it was universally acknowledged that George Thomas was one in a million.

JACKIE WILSON

Born 1936

Farmer

Tully Beg, Rathmelton, County Donegal

At the age of twenty, Jackie Wilson decided he'd had enough. All his life, the soft-spoken Ulsterman had attended the Presbyterian Church in Rathmelton and listened dutifully as the various ministers lectured and berated the congregation on the evil ways of the world. His fellow worshippers descended from men and women who had been meeting here since the 1630s when Robert Pont, a grandson of John Knox, was its first minister.

But for Jackie, the Presbyterian outlook on life just wasn't hitting the right spot. It was 1956 and music was taking over. Elvis was wooing America with 'Hound Dog' and 'Blue Suede Shoes'. Another Jackie Wilson was telling the world that 'Your love keeps lifting me higher'. Cinemas across Ireland were showing musicals like *Carousel* and *The King and I*. And the first *Eurovision Song Contest* was broadcast from Switzerland. Everywhere Jackie looked, people wanted to sing.

It was at about this time that Jackie was 'born again' and began to worship at the Pentecostal Church in Letterkenny. Over half a century later, Jackie is one of the Pentecostal regulars, taking his seat at eleven o'clock every Sunday morning. The 150-strong congregation comprises people of every colour and creed, and includes many children. 'We are all one,' explains Jackie. 'You pray for your friends and for your folks but it's all about prayers from the heart. It's a much more direct experience.' The service lasts for two hours and involves a good deal of singing, sometimes accompanied by guitars. Many of the hymns were written by Methodists such as Charles Gabriel, author of one of Jackie's favourites, 'I Stand Amazed in the Presence of Jesus the Nazarene'. But there are also a number of new hymns aimed at the younger generation. After the service, members intermingle over coffee and tea. The whole experience impressed Jackie so much that he named his two-storey farmhouse Emmanuel, meaning 'God with Us'.

Jackie's farm straddles a beautiful rolling landscape a few miles west of Rathmelton. He inherited it upon the death of his ninety-one-year-old father, Thomas. The Wilsons came from Scotland in the early seventeenth century and Jackie's grandfather, Johnny Wilson, married a girl from Enniskillen and ran a small farm near The Breen in Rathmelton.

In 1959, Jackie's father expanded the family assets with the purchase of 150 acres of the Swiney estate at Tullybeg. This was the farm that Jackie, the eldest of six, inherited and which he now runs with his own son, Jonathan. Jackie was, perhaps, lucky to inherit anything from his father as many Presbyterians would have seen his conversion as an act of betrayal. 'My father wasn't too happy at the time but he understood,' says Jackie. 'And my mother didn't mind so long as I was going to some church.' Talking to those who know Jackie, it is unsurprising he managed to win back his parents. He is variously described as 'extraordinarily giving', 'non-judgemental', 'watchful', 'protective' and 'wise'.

While Jonathan looks after the cattle and sheep today, Jackie keeps a close eye on the poultry, namely some forty chickens and ducks who waddle around a small, enclosed orchard of 200-year-old apple trees. They are fed potatoes, grown on the farm and cooked in a giant pot that bubbles on the kitchen Rayburn all day long. Jackie sells the eggs to neighbours and, occasionally, a luckless drake might fetch up on the dinner table.

A nearby Nissen Hut opens out into a slightly sloping meadow where a dozen lean, white-faced Texel ewes are grazing. Every night, the sheep make their way into the hut to sleep. In another field, thirty beef cattle fatten on the grass in advance of their trek to the market at Carrigans. They are primarily black Aberdeen Angus and pure white Charolais. Beside the cattle byre, twenty large black silage bags have been daubed with white paint in the shape of a cross. Jackie says the paint keeps scavenging rooks and jackdaws at bay as it creates an illusion that there are other, bigger birds parping on these bags. It sounds far-fetched until you see the silhouettes of a hundred crow's nests in the treetops and note that the silage bags are parp-free.

Jackie says the landscape of his farm has not changed in fifty years – though it feels as if it has been like this for at least 300. The trees are ancient, elms, beech and sycamore, although Hurricane Debbie devastated the woods back in 1961. The sounds are familiar – a startled rooster, a bleating lamb, a swinging gate. In an old cobblestone shed, a grey Massey 135 stands at ease. 'I used to plough with horses,' says Jackie, 'but then we got this wee girl.' While we eye it up, Jackie's dog Rover hops up and takes the seat. The tractor tour of the farm with Jackie is evidently the highlight of Rover's day. 'I didn't know anything about how they worked when we got her,' continues Jackie, 'but she's a great old tractor and I wouldn't swap her for a new one.'

In 1965, a Faith Missionary friend from Duncannon introduced Jackie to her sister Phyllis. 'And that,' laughs Jackie, 'is how you get caught up.' He and Phyllis were married soon after and had six children. They lost their second child to a rare blood disorder some years ago. But, with eleven grandchildren and counting, Jackie is confident that 'the Wilson name is not going to die out in a hurry'.

CATHY DOWLING

Born 1917

Market Gardener

Ballyburn, Castledermot, County Carlow

In 1935, the Public Dance Halls Act banned the practice of house dances in Ireland. The Catholic Church considered them immoral. These private 'at home' dances essentially consisted of sets (four couples) or half-sets (two couples) dancing to quadrilles, a lively and intricate dance introduced to Ireland by veterans of the Napoleonic Wars and adapted to Irish music over the course of the nineteenth century. Indeed, if you were looking for love before 1935, then a house dance was probably the best place to go.

Not everyone kowtowed after the ban. House dances continued during the Emergency Years of the Second World War and it was at one such dance that Cathy Murphy met Billy Dowling, the father of her four children and her husband for fifty-seven years.

'There used to be nothing only dances in the houses,' she laughs. 'We had some neighbours and great friends, two girls, who worked in Dublin. When they came home, they'd have a dance and we'd go all night. The two girls got married on the same day and there was a fierce crowd in the house, fifty or sixty people. It went on through until five or six o'clock in the morning. I don't know how people had the energy. There was no drink at that time. It was just an accordion and a violin and the people dancing on the cement floor.'

Cathy was born in 1917, the second in a family of five. Her father, Dan Murphy, was a young man when his father died, leaving him a forty-acre farm at Collin, just south of the village of Moone in County Kildare. Dan's grandfather had leased the land from the Leonard family of Hill View. During the 1930s, the Land Commission appropriated the farm and offered it to Dan. 'He was a terrible honest man and he said he didn't make much money and he'd never be able to pay for it,' recalls Cathy. 'My mother was raging with him! She was very industrious and hard working!' One way or another, the Murphys secured the land which Cathy's only brother, also Dan, farms today.

Cathy's mother, Kate Murphy, had a sister who lost her husband at an early age. With only one young baby to rear, the concern was that Kate's sister would become lonesome. Kate's solution was to send her eldest daughter, Molly, to live with the widow. And Molly remained with her aunt 'all the time until she grew up and got a job'. Despite the fact that the house was only a few fields away from the Murphys, Cathy came to see Molly more as a cousin than a sister 'because she was always over there'.

Cathy herself spent four of her earliest years living with another aunt at Talbotstown, near Baltinglass, County Wicklow. 'Everyone was very poor at that time,' she explains. 'There was no money and people had to work hard. They only survived, that's all. Still, everyone was happy. They had no money. But now, they all have money and maybe they're not as happy.'

When Cathy was ten, her younger sister contracted measles and died. 'When people got sick that time, there was really nowhere to go. We had the doctor come but there wasn't the medication for her. She was always very delicate. And you couldn't have the doctor coming all the time. He lived a long way away from them. People wouldn't be using doctors either. They'd be going to different people for different things. Like if they had shingles, they'd go to the quacks who'd try and cure them.'

Life expectancy was very different then, says Cathy, and 'seventy [years] was the best you'd hope for'. 'But there were the odd ones who lived a long time.' Her neighbours included a couple called Mr and Mrs Dunne who lived to be ninety-three and ninety-four. 'I knew them from the time I was a child, so they must have been born in the 1830s. They were a great old pair, very light-hearted. They'd sit by the open fire and he'd be tormenting her about being such an auld woman – and the two of them the same age!'

Cathy's childhood was fundamentally cheerful. Her mother taught them card games and took them to whist drives. Her uncle regaled them with stories until midnight. Her father played fiddle and explained the rules of the GAA. Much to his delight, Kildare reached the All-Ireland football final five times between 1926 and 1931 – and won twice. Cathy often accompanied her father and brother to the teacher's house in Moone, where they would huddle around a wireless, listening as the points and goals clocked up. 'And that was nearly eighty years ago,' she marvels.

By day, Cathy helped her parents on the farm, tending to the pigs and crops, 'a small bit of corn, a few potatoes and some turnips'. When her mother prepared the donkey for the weekly shopping trips to Moore's grocery in Grangecon or to visit the fair in Baltinglass, Cathy and her sisters would leap up on the cart alongside her. 'It was all donkeys and ponies and traps then,' she recalls, 'or else you walked.' For a long time, the priest was the only man around who had a car. Even Mr Leonard of Hill View travelled by bicycle. When one of her uncles had a sick cow, his only option was to walk all the way to the town of Athy to inform the vet, a five-hour round trip.

Cathy was in her early twenties when she became the proud owner of her own black High Nellie bicycle. 'That was a great gift!' she says. 'God, I often cycled down to cousins in Tinahely and I used to stay there a couple of days. There was no traffic on the roads. No cars. A few bicycles and people walking and maybe the farmers would be taking the cattle into the market.' Much as she loved cycling, she cannot recommend the busy roads of modern Ireland as a sensible place for bicycles. She does, however, favour the commendable proposition to reopen the country's disused railways as bicycle tracks.

Cathy was thirty-four years old when she met the late William 'Billy' Dowling of Ballyhade, County Carlow, at a house dance. They were married in Moone in 1951. In the absence of her father, who died in 1934, she was given away by her brother, Dan. The newlyweds duly purchased a forty-eight-acre farm at Ballyburn and set up a clever and somewhat pioneering business, growing top-quality vegetables – 'carrots, potatoes, cabbage, scallions, onions, strawberries and all'. Assisted by their three sons and one daughter, they would gather, wash, weigh and pack the vegetables at the house and then Billy would drive them into Carlow, where he stocked eight shops. 'He worked hard at it, but he made good money,' says Seamus, Billy and Cathy's eldest son. The house where the Dowlings raised their family stands behind a modern bungalow where Cathy lives today. Billy passed away in 2008 at the age of ninety-two, leaving her with 'many happy memories'.

JOHNNY FYFE

Born 1930

Farm Manager / Gardener

Killegar, County Leitrim

Johnny Fyfe gazes around the yard of Killegar and says nothing at all. The decline began the night of the fire – and that was nearly forty years ago. Before that, these crumbling walls echoed with activity. Beneath the arch is the stable where they kept the horse traps. Another bricked-up doorway marks the entrance to the workhorse stable. Over there was the cattle byre. It's full of twisted, wet old logs now. And up there you can see where the lads hoisted grain sacks into the loft. He hesitates before leading us out to the old Laundry Green, where the sheets and pillowcases of the Big House were hung out to dry in the summers of his youth. 'The lord would take a notion sometimes,' he warns.

During the early 1960s, the 3rd Lord Kilbracken, owner of Killegar, began to plant trees with a passion. He believed they would provide his heirs with a valuable source of income for generations to come. No part of the lord's estate was safe from cultivation. The best fields, the back lawns, the kitchen garden, even the tennis court was planted. So, too, was the Laundry Green, although the Norway spruces that stood here have been felled recently. Prematurely, in Johnny's view. The contractors who cleared it have left behind a wild, uncompromising confusion of briary bushes, amputated stumps and distorted limbs. Johnny Fyfe sighs wearily. I get the impression that he often sighs wearily and that he may have done so for the best part of eighty years.

When Johnny was born in 1930, his father ran a small farm near Ballyconnell, County Cavan, and operated as a thatcher in the locality. The farm belonged to Johnny's mother's people and perhaps old Mr Fyfe was never quite at ease there. In 1942, the 2nd Lord Kilbracken offered him a job as head gardener at the Killegar estate just across the Leitrim border. Lord Kilbracken's father had been Gladstone's private secretary and India's longest-serving Under Secretary of State. His grandfather founded Christchurch in New Zealand.

Mr Fyfe's wife, Jean-Anne, was simultaneously appointed cook. The Fyfes duly took up residence in the small gardener's cottage where Johnny still lives today. By the age of twelve, Johnny was working alongside his father, sowing, weeding, gathering fruit and vegetables. At its peak, the garden could cater for the biggest shooting parties that Lord Kilbracken threw. Potatoes, cabbages, lettuce and onions arose from the nutritious earth. There were plums and gooseberries, pears and apples, and a grapevine that clambered around the greenhouse walls. People came from miles around to buy the Killegar strawberries.

In 1950, eight years after the Fyfes arrived at Killegar, the 2nd lord passed away and his thirty-year-old son, John, inherited the 600-acre estate. The young lord had piloted a Fairey Swordfish for the Fleet Air Arm throughout the Second World War. He now rolled up his sleeves and gave his all to ensure Killegar prospered. During the harvest, he often drove the combine and, when the threshing was complete, he threw a large hooley at the Big House for the seasonal labourers. Amongst the lively recitations to echo down the corridors on such nights was Johnny Fyfe's rendition of 'The Boys of the County Armagh'.

The moody, ivy-clad mansion of Killegar House was built at the end of the Napoleonic Wars, high above the waters of Lough Kilnemar. Johnny and the lord were the only two people in the house on the night of the fire in 1970, the cause of which is unknown. A lit cigarette butt prematurely flung into a waste-paper basket by his lordship? Or perhaps the basket was simply too close to the gas fire. At any rate, the fire gutted the house and severely dented Lord Kilbracken's soul.

His passion for planting trees evolved. They were arboreal lightweights for the most part – poplars (for matchsticks), black alder (for compost) and willows (for wood-pellet stoves). Johnny was always sceptical. 'If I was going out to get a bit of wood for the fire, I wouldn't be going for willow.'

At length, Lord Kilbracken's eyes fell upon the pasturelands of Killegar and he decided to plant them with trees too. And so the hundred-strong herd of pedigree cattle had to go. This was particularly devastating to Johnny, who had helped build up the herd over two decades. He often accompanied Lord Kilbracken to the Spring Show in Dublin to watch these handsome Herefords and Shorthorns on parade. Johnny trained the bulls up from the time they were calves. When they became obstreperous yearlings, he was the one who wrestled them into submission. Johnny was always an enthusiast for shooting. During Killegar's shooting season, he led the beaters through the thickets, spiralling pheasant and woodcock into the dangerous sky. 'I was a keen shot too,' he says.

Inevitably, Johnny and Kilbracken began to disagree. 'It was very hard to make money out of the place the way he was doing it. He thought he knew all about farming and that's why me and him fell out latterly.'

For many years after, Johnny found employment elsewhere, in sawmills and forests 'all over Ireland'. The 3rd lord passed away in 2006 and the estate awaits its future with uncertainty. Johnny continues to work part time at Killegar.

By day, this modest, soft-spoken, solitary man often takes his boat up the quiet Killegar River. Mollie, his young spaniel, is always by his side. On these still waters, Johnny casts his rod in pursuit of pike, perch and the occasional trout. He says that when the water is high enough, you could row up to Donegal. But the salmon that spawned here in Novembers past never get this far upriver anymore. The night-poachers who once came here with pitchforks no longer bother.

In the evenings, Johnny might pop into Charles Farrelly's in Carrigallen for a nightcap. Otherwise, he is most at ease in his own cottage, seated by the solid fuel burner that heats room, radiator and bath water. Along his walls are his dart trophies and a series of photographs of trusty spaniels since departed.

One of the photos shows a spaniel slumped across the seat of a BSA 150 motorbike. 'I got that brand new in 1957 and I paid for it with rabbits,' says Johnny. For every rabbit he brought to the butcher, he would earn half a crown. Thirty-six half-crowns (or thirty-six dead rabbits) was the equivalent of his weekly wage of £4.50 at Killegar. 'I had it paid for in eleven months,' he says. It's not clear how many rabbits the bike cost but, given the appalling effects of myxomatosis in the area, he'd have been hard pushed to achieve that today. 'The rabbits are all gone now,' sighs Johnny wearily.

TIMMY & STEVIE KELLEHER

Born 1925 and 1930

Farmer and Hackney Driver

Dingle, County Kerry

There has been much talk in recent years about the clampdown on drink-driving and how it has played havoc with the traditional pub-going routine of Ireland's rural community. Bachelor brothers Stevie and Timmy Kelleher have a canny solution to the problem. Even though their farm is less than three kilometres from their preferred pubs in Dingle town, they know better than to risk driving home 'after a few'. Stevie was a hackney driver for many decades and respects the rules of the road. 'If I was put off the road,' he says, 'I may as well hang up my boots and die.'

The Kellehers' answer to the drink-driving conundrum is to have two houses – a farmhouse, where they spend most of their days, and a townhouse in Dingle, where they rest on drinking nights. 'We go out four nights a week and we stay in town then,' says Stevie. 'We went out last night because the night before was very windy and I didn't close an eye. So I said to Timmy, "We'll go to town tonight and have a couple of drinks and we'll stay in town and we'll sleep."'

'Going out' is arguably the reason why neither of these courteous, open-minded men is married. 'And thanks be to Christ for that,' they say in unison. 'We wouldn't be as happy as we are now,' believes Stevie. 'We can do what we like and go where we like and no one will say a word.'

Stevie is the younger brother by five years. He is a hearty gabbler and his anecdotes are delivered in a frenetic Kerry accent that makes every sentence seem more real, more raw and often a good deal more funny. He is not without opinion and quickly launches a volley of tirades against anything from Dublin's gangsters (a 'cowardly shower' hiding behind guns and knives) to the bankers who allowed young couples 'to be sunk up to their necks in debt for the rest of their lives'.

While Stevie rarely draws breath, Timmy is the quiet man. He tends to sit with his chin cupped in a hand, nodding along. He enjoys talking about the weather. Sometimes, he sings 'about old times and everything'.

Their mother, Hannah, was the third of four daughters born to Timothy Kennedy, a devout Catholic who farmed amid the megalithic cairns and standing stones of Coumduff, above Anascaul. All four Kennedy daughters entered arranged marriages. 'It was all matches at that time,' explains Stevie. 'You had

to have a fortune – a couple of hundred pounds – and then you could get married.' Hannah was also deeply religious, permanently mumbling the Hail Mary and the Our Father. Her legacy lives on in her sons who attend mass regularly and kneel down after supper every evening to say the Rosary.

In 1923, Hannah married Thomas Kelleher, a forty-year-old farmer from Milltown, west of Dingle. Three sons and two daughters followed. Stevie, the youngest son, says it was a difficult childhood. 'Poor people didn't have any money,' he says. 'And I don't know how our parents fed us but they did. 'Tis great the way it is today but – and I've said this in pubs – the youth of today wouldn't do what we did. They'd die with the hunger.'

In the 'great summer' of 1937, Thomas Kelleher converted his late father's thatched cottage into the dark, grey, two-storey farmhouse where his sons live today. A decade later, he died of a heart attack at the age of sixty-three.

While Timmy took on the farm, Hannah set Stevie and her daughters up with mortgages. Stevie became a hackney driver and cleared his mortgage inside a year and a half. 'When I started on the road, there were no jobs around here and money was very scarce. But I worked hard and I drove twenty hours out of twenty-four and I lost a lot of sleep.'

In 1950, Stevie bought a thirty-two-horsepower V8, black as night, from the Walden Motor Company on Parnell Street in Dublin. 'Jesus, the power of it!' he recalls. He secured it for a good price when the garage mechanic tipped him off that the salesman liked a drink. His driving took him all over Ireland. As a farmer, he was captivated by the pasturelands of Kildare and Meath. 'We call that the long grass country.' He hated cities and met some unspeakably rude people along the way. One person even accused him of 'being a Corkman'.

In 1968, David Lean and his crew arrived in Dingle to film the epic *Ryan's Daughter*. 'Heir of Christ!' exclaims Stevie. 'That's forty years ago now, is it?' The film changed the lives of everyone in the town. 'There wasn't a restaurant in Dingle before that time,' says Timmy. 'You couldn't get a cup of tea. And the pubs were empty except for a few locals.' By 1969, he was working as a full-time chauffeur to Peter Dukelow, the film's hard-drinking construction manager. The film did not fare well at the US box office but Dingle certainly got a mighty boost from the publicity.

In later years, Stevie drove a truck for a local supermarket, P.&T. FitzGerald (now a Centra), and took bus tours around the dancehalls and old-time pubs of Munster. 'Stevie's Bus', as it was known, also wheeled its way around the Ring of Kerry once a week, '186 miles, the round trip'.

Meanwhile, young Timmy was running the fifty-acre farm, milking and feeding a herd of fifteen cattle. During the 1970s, he began to breed ponies and the Kellehers have become icons on Kerry's racing circuit, famed from the beaches of Billbawn and Glenbeigh to the tracks of Caherciveen and Castleisland. 'I don't know how we got into them,' says Stevie. 'But we were always mad for the ponies.' The brothers bred their own, trained them up and fed them with oats from the farm. Timmy proved a formidable jockey and won seven races, most famously on Jet Black, the enigmatically named grey who won the trophy that stands today upon the Kelleher mantelpiece. 'I cycled back that day and she followed me on my bike all eight miles home,' adds Timmy.

Photographs of these victorious steeds are pinned upon the tobacco-stained, tongue-and-groove walls of their living room. Above the dresser, the Sacred Heart, bedecked in sprigs of holly all year round, jostles for space between faded snaps of Stevie's beloved V8, the Eucharistic Congress of 1932 and cloth-capped friends from decades gone by. The brothers sit in well-worn armchairs either side of the stove, boots resting on a black stone floor. 'Ah we're used to this way,' says Stevie. 'And it will do us all right. Will you be in Dingle for a drink later?'

JOE MULDOON

Born 1931

Farmer

Ballymote, County Sligo

'There's been worse times than this, that's for sure,' says Joe Muldoon. 'And so long as you have a bit to eat, the price of a pint and a bed to lie in, then what about it? Let tomorrow be the worser day.'

We met him first in Hayden's of Lord Edward Street, arguably the handsomest bar in Ballymote, dressed in a dapper suit with a long, dark overcoat and a fine cap. He comes here every Wednesday evening to drink a few black stouts and listen to the traditional music session that commences shortly after nine o'clock. He invited us out to his farm the next time we were passing through.

Three weeks later, Joe Muldoon is standing out in his field with a scythe. He wears a long khaki jacket, held tight by baler twine. The weather is about to turn and he's slightly breathless. He's been clearing rushes out from the ditch and the hawthorn bushes that mark the boundary of his land. 'You sleep well after a day out with this,' he says, tapping his scythe. 'There's not many to work it, bar myself.' He bids us in from this increasingly dirty day and we move towards the 1950s cottage where he eats and sleeps. Built by the council, Joe bought it for himself a quarter of a century ago. 'It's my own now anyway,' he says. 'I can't be put out of it.'

Joe was born on another farm in 1931. 'The old place', as he calls it, was a pretty farmstead in Rathdoony More, a few miles northwest of Ballymote. It belonged to his mother's people, Rooneys. Joe's father Patrick Muldoon was an elderly man when he married his third wife, Kate Rooney. It was rare in such times for a man to have been married twice before but any children from these marriages emigrated to America long before Joe was born. He believes his half-brother may have died in the trenches during the First World War. Joe does not know what his grandparents did – he never met any of them – but assumes his family have farmed for many generations.

Kate Muldoon bore her husband three strapping sons, Paddy, Sonny (John Patrick) and Joe. In 1933, when Joe was two, his father availed of the terms of the new Land Act to purchase five-and-a-half acres just outside Ballymote from the Land Commission. This land, where Joe lives today, was previously part of the estate of Captain Gethin, the land agent to the Gore-Booth family. 'He owned all this land one time,' says Joe, 'from Ballymote to the butt of the hill.' Joe recalls this area being one large woodland in his youth but, after the Land Commission acquired it, they sold the trees, which were harvested by Regan's Sawmills of Ballymote.

Patrick Muldoon was all set to convert his new land into a small, working farm when he was taken ill with kidney trouble and died in 1935. His widow took their three young sons to live with her bachelor brother at 'the old place' at Rathdoony by Temple House Lake.

The school where the Muldoon boys learned to read and write has long since been demolished. It was a solitary cottage in the village of Emlaghnaghtan, run by kindly Miss Kilcoyne from Tobercurry and 'a thundering bulldozer' called Mr Cassidy. Joe says the latter man was always pulling ears and whacking children with his cane. One time, he 'threw the full fist into the side of my face and splayed blood up onto the roof'. Kate Muldoon hurled a scalding torrent of words at the teacher. Revenge became rather more physical when Joe, aged twenty-one – and with 'a good few scoops of porter' on board – encountered Cassidy at a céilí and let loose with his fists.

For all that, Joe is a peaceful man. When he talks, his eyes light up every wrinkle upon his face. He speaks earnestly and importantly, and enjoys a good laugh. He drinks calmly and smokes a couple of a John Players after he's had his tea.

When Joe's mother died in 1967, his elder brother Paddy succeeded to the seventeen-and-a-half acre farm at Rathdoony. Sonny, who had served in the Irish army, was working as a postman in Tullamore, where he lived until his death in 1982. Joe decided to take on his father's field at Ballymote and see what he could make of it. The land was still full of stumps when he arrived, the legacy of Regan's blades. 'But I took out all the butts,' says Joe. 'I spent days out there pulling out the roots, every beech and fir. I got down and take the hatchet to them. That was hard work all right, and it took time to change it, but I got there.' Paddy and Joe then joined forces, building up a herd of thirty-five cattle which they grazed on their respective lands. Every now and then they would bring some heifers into the Thursday market in Ballymote and see what price they could get. Generally, that gave them enough to live on but 1975 was 'a bad old year'. 'You couldn't sell a cow at all,' he says.

When Paddy succumbed to cancer in 1995, Joe succeeded to his land. He sold the bulk of it on, retaining an eight-acre field where, today, he keeps a dozen heifers. He also inherited the thatched farmhouse and successfully applied for a Section 5 grant 'to get the iron' on the roof.

Joe Muldoon was married twice. His first wife was Miss Bridie Murphy from Riverstown but she was taken ill early in the marriage, before they had any children. 'She died in England,' he says quietly. 'Her sister came back from America and took her over there to see a faith healer. It was as well to let me run this country, but she left in November and I did not see her and she died on 3 March 1978.'

In April 1979, he married Margaret 'but it didn't work'. They had one daughter, Catherine, born in 1980, who represents the solitary Muldoon of her generation. A trainee childcare supervisor, she has inherited her father's shining eyes and regularly visits him with her Lithuanian boyfriend and her two sons. Although she grew up on her father's farm and misses the peace of the countryside, Catherine now describes herself as 'a townie'.

'When the weather gets good in the month of April, I will be away with the lads cutting turf on the bog,' says Joe. That is about as far as he will go. He has never left Ireland and only visited Dublin once.

'To get him as far as Sligo is a challenge,' interjects Catherine. One technical flaw to travelling is that Joe does not drive. He gets about on a rusty-belled High Nellie bike or avails of lifts from kindly neighbours. In the good old days, he kept a small herd of donkeys and went about on a cart, gathering turf and hay. 'But with the way the traffic is now, you can't go out on the road like that or you'll be killed,' he warns.

JOHN CARSON

Born 1928

Farmer

Isle View, Inishmore, County Fermanagh

The 2,500-acre island of Inishmore emerges from the upper reaches of Lough Erne. Rainbows arch over its grassy drumlins and slate-grey streams. Roads wobble uncertainly along the boggy earth. Cattle meander through misty meadows and survey the fine views without any apparent interest.

There is history a-plenty on Inishmore, from the tenth-century standing stone to the ruins of a white-washed cottage stripped back to its bare bricks in 1822 by the bullets that whizzed between Catholics and Protestants in a gun battle known as the Inishmore Fight. John Carson's uncle once witnessed a gypsy woman having a baby on the side of the road near here while her family carried on about their business all around her. 'There was no more remarks passed than if a cow was calving,' he said.

John's father and uncle moved to the island when they bought a farm in 1918. Farming was in the Carson blood at least since their forbears left the fertile fields of Devon in the late seventeenth century. They first settled at Garrison on the banks of Lough Melvin, which forms the Sligo–Fermanagh border. During the 1860s, John's great-grandfather broke away and moved first to Letterbreen and then on to Kinawley, always in pursuit of better land.

John's grandfather, also called John, had farmed pigs in Kinawley, bringing them to the market in Enniskillen. Fair Day in Enniskillen was a lively affair but many a farmer was bankrupted by swiping hands amid the jostling crowds. To confound the pickpockets, Granny Carson made her husband a special wallet to keep in his crotch. The younger John tells the story of an old neighbour who had a similarly located purse, although his was designed to protect his fortune from his two insatiably drunken sisters. 'This man subsequently fell in love with a pretty girl and told her of his wealth. "Aye," said she, "I hear the bee but where's the honey?" The man said back to her, "Put your hand down there and you'll find all the honey you need."'

Old John Carson found the land in Kinawley 'terrible heavy' to farm pigs. With his young family growing fast, he needed a quicker income and so he took to building roads. In 1897, he found work along-side a Scottish engineer who was employed to build a new viaduct linking Inishmore to the 'mainland'. It wasn't an easy job. The foundations kept sinking into the bog, no matter how many carts of stone and clay his men brought in. The Scotsman gave up and a new engineer arrived with a wily solution, namely securing the base with hessian sacks of cement. Grandfather Carson helped make those sacks and you can still see them at the foot of the viaduct today.

In 1926, John's father, Hugh, married Miss Chamber of Mackan Glebe and brought her back to this island. Born in 1928, John was the first of their three sons. Like most children on the island, he attended the now-ruined Methodist school at Slee, established during the Great Famine. John's aunt was the teacher. A photograph from 1934 shows the young lad smiling with his school pals. Sometimes, they would go out and catch the pike as they were 'schooling'. They'd gather the fish in loops, behead them, salt them, dry them and sell them by the dozen. If many of the boys in the photo look alike it is perhaps because 'one family had seventeen children in it'. At that time, just twenty-six families lived on the island. John does not know how many live there today but new-builds have been advancing steadily towards his farm for many years now.

John Carson left school in 1944 to help on the farm. The following year, his father dislocated a hip when a horse reared on him. 'He was never able to work at the markets after that and had a terrible pain for the rest of his days.'

Meanwhile, John's somewhat contrary bachelor uncle put his part of the farm up for sale. The seventeen-year-old realised his time had come and bought his uncle's farm. It took him five years to pay it off.

By the age of twenty-two, John was effectively running the eighty-acre Carson farm. What was missing? The older generation shook their heads. 'You're too young,' they said. Florence was nineteen years old. They were married in Maguire's Bridge in 1952 and went on to have six daughters and a son. It was a very happy marriage and lasted nearly fifty years until Florence's death in 2001. Their first grandson was born in Australia on her first anniversary, an event that greatly moved John.

John is an expressive man, with a kindly, crinkly face. Photographs mean a lot to him. They hang on walls, stand upon shelves and sleep in albums in every room of the house. We flick through an album. There's his parents, standing straight, out by the old house. And that's wee William, his younger brother, who 'died last harvest'. Here we have a smattering of his grandchildren, scattered through the latitudes these days from New Zealand to Belfast. The young ones come up to play on the farm sometimes, pow-pow gun-games behind the cattle troughs, sliding in the muddy lanes. And there's his daughter and her husband, the one who was injured during the Remembrance Day bomb blast in Enniskillen back in 1987. And there's John, in his UDR uniform, attending the funeral of Jimmy Graham, one of three brothers gunned down in the 1980s.

When John talks of the bad times, his voice becomes suddenly sterner, his sentences brusquer, his posture stiffer. 'It's still there at the back of the whole thing,' he says. 'And it always will be.' He was nineteen when he joined the B-Specials of the Home Guard and he stayed with them for twenty-two years. During that time, they went head-to-head against the IRA in an aggressive border campaign that the B-Specials eventually won. That said, John says he had a relatively peaceful time and 'never saw anyone insulted or upset'. After the B-Specials were disbanded in 1967, John joined the Ulster Defence Regiment with whom he remained with for the next ten years. He is considerably more open than many on the subject but it is still not an area he feels comfortable talking about.

During his time, John built up a herd of pedigree black Aberdeen Angus from thirty to a couple of hundred. Twice a year, he brought them into Enniskillen, a long ten-mile march to the bridge and onwards up the main road. 'It was awful if you didn't sell them and had to walk them home again.' Today, he and his son Robert farm seventy cows, half milk, half sucklers. Back in the 1940s, his father would go to hiring fairs to recruit sturdy young fellows who wanted a few months' work. Today, it is just the Carsons, another young lad and three Massey Fergusons.

NOEL ROBINSON

Born 1939

Farmer

Coole, County Westmeath

'They're headed for the Hill of Maol,' says Noel Robinson, watching the drakes in flight. 'Ducks have to fly backwards over Maol,' he explains, 'to keep the dust from going into their eyes.'

At least that's what the late Tommy Riggs told him. Tommy was an old man who lived up the road. He knew all there was to know about these parts and could bring you 'back to the day he was born'. He made a fortune out of rabbits during the Second World War, gathering them up on a horse and cart and dispatching them to the ration-ravaged butchers of England. In 1950, which was the last year he dealt in rabbits, Tommy recorded a staggering 64,000 on his books. Most were caught in snares and traps, though some were pounced upon by ferrets hidden at the burrow mouths. 'You had to be careful with ferrets though,' recalls Noel. 'Sometimes they'd go down and kill the rabbit and eat it and fall asleep. Then you were left without ferret or rabbit.' Snares and ferrets may have been 'rather cruel', he concedes, but 'at that time, the money was unreal'. Rabbits made five shillings a head, and five rabbits was the equivalent of a farm labourer's weekly wage.

Noel's farm has been in the family for more generations than anyone can remember. The Robinsons started out as tenants of the Pakenham family of Pakenham Hall, now Tullynally Castle. By 1874, Noel's great-grandfather had amassed nearly 100 acres. That year, he built the stone farmhouse where Noel's son now lives.

Noel's father, John Robinson, spent some time in America as a young man, principally in Buffalo, New York. In 1927, he returned to Ireland to take on the family farm. Eleven years later, John married Margaret Doherty, a Catholic from nearby Williamstown. The mixed marriage caused 'holy desolation' in both the Protestant and Catholic communities. His father was obliged to sign papers vowing that his children would be raised as Catholics. He says that things have moved on a good deal since. Not so long ago, a priest went around the houses urging his flock not to attend a mixed wedding in the locality. 'Of course we all went in force, and on time,' says Noel. 'That's enough of that bullshite.'

On 3 January 1953, the children of Ireland went back to school. Noel, who turned fourteen that day, did not join them. Instead he quit school and went to help his ailing father on the farm. 'John Robsinson

55

was a big strong man,' says Noel. 'Six foot one and a physique to go with it.' But during the early 1950s, 'he got crippled with arthritis and ran into all sorts of hardship – diabetes and a stroke and, in the heel of the hunt, the whole system just caved in'.

At this time, John was also running a second farm of 411 acres which he had inherited from his Uncle Willy in 1951. However, as news of his poor health spread, the Land Commission swooped down with a compulsory purchase order. The 411 acres became £15,000 in land bonds. 'That would have been good enough, if you got the money, but it ended up the land bonds weren't worth the paper they were written on.'

In 1961, twenty-two-year-old Noel went to see his dying father in a hospital in Dublin and learned that he was to inherit the family farm, 'lock, stock and barrel'. John died in November 1966 and, as Noel says, he's been 'stuck with it since'. 'Not that I made such a good job of it but I still have it.'

Noel's farm forms a square of good pastureland to the rear of the farmyard. 'This is about the only farm around here that has been continuously worked by the one family all along,' says Noel. Most of his neighbours have sold up or rented their land out. His cattle are 'a sort of a mix' of a breed and he has a bull running around and 'there could be any sort in it'. He brings them to market locally or to the factory in Ballyjamesduff. There is also a flock of forty ewes and lambs, spread across a grassy meadow beside his house. Sheltered beneath a band of trees, a large pond provides a popular retreat for wild ducks.

In a nearby field at Turbotstown, there is a holy well. A survey of Ireland in the 1940s estimated that there were upwards of 3,000 sacred wells on this island, far more than any other country. There is something defiantly, anciently otherworld about holy wells. The Turbotstown well is a very small affair, known as a rose well. A bucket of water would empty it. And yet it has never dried up. A whitethorn bush stands guard alongside. When Noel was young, the bush was covered in ribbons, tied on by those who came to pray. 'But I think the only ribbons on it now are the ones I put there,' he says. 'I believe in those things because why else should there be a well out there in the middle of nowhere? There is seemingly no spring in it, but there's always water in it.'

The future for Noel's farm is 'hard to predict'. He has two sons but believes farming is of limited appeal to either of them. Holding such a deep-rooted passion for the farm, his greatest fear is that it will be sold to someone else and that he will be prohibited from walking across the land. 'After seventy years, that's what I would be afraid of. I always have that at the back of my mind.'

MICK KING

Born 1924

Farmer

Lanmore, County Mayo

'I don't know whose land it was to begin with. It might have been the devil's for all I know.' Mick King is speaking of the thirty-seven-acre farm at which he was born eighty-five years ago and where he has lived for the vast majority of his life. Located on a rugged hillside some five miles south of Westport, the farm belonged to his mother's people, the Hanlons. He has vague recollections of his mother's mother, who lived with them during the 1920s. 'A grand old woman', clad in black, although he was so young when she died that 'if she had a pair of horns, I mightn't have taken a bit of notice of her'. The farmstead has changed little since his childhood save that the ancient sheds, once thatched, are now corrugated.

Mick's father grew up on a farm six miles away in Drummin. 'Well, I wouldn't call it a farm,' counters Mick. 'It was a bloody mountain place … but they had plenty of fields for the sheep.' Cousins have since sold the land and moved to England. 'And I wouldn't blame them,' he adds.

He is a quiet gentleman with a sharp, old-fashioned wit. When he heard about the Californian woman who had octuplets, he retorted, 'Lord, she must be like a sausage-making machine.' When he sees a sample portrait of himself on James's camera, he whistles, 'I don't look too bad at all. I'm like a Reverend Mother. I'd turn a few [heads] on the road anyway.'

He went to a school in nearby Lankill where 'swallows flew in and out the broken windows' and 'you'd clap your hands every now and then to stay warm'. Like many in those days, he brought his own turf for the school hearth but 'the master would soon have his big backside up to it, taking all the heat'. Mick left school at fourteen and went to help his father on the farm.

England has always had a certain allure for Mick. One of the few times he saw Dublin was when he caught a ferry from the North Wall to England. 'I just took a notion to go,' he says. 'There were plenty from around here who were there then.' In London, where his sisters lived, he found work laying electricity cables in the north of the city. It was a long, long way from Mayo to Cricklewood but Mick reckons he was 'settling in nicely'. And then he got a call from his father, summoning him back to the farm.

London was not the only place to which Mick escaped. When he was twenty-eight, he saw an advertisement from the Electricity Supply Board seeking workers for its new power station at Allenwood

in County Kildare. And so he followed the path of many from the west and went to work for the summer in the Bog of Allen, cutting turf for the station. The men slept in 'the best of huts' by Allenwood Cross and worked hard. 'You wouldn't like to be too long on the bogs,' he counsels. Not all of the turf they cut went to the ESB. Some was barged off down the Grand Canal to Dublin and more went by lorry to the big towns of Leinster. The nightlife was feisty in Allenwood and Mick admits he did not keep too much change from his time there. 'I often put away eight or nine [pints] in a night,' he says.

'Do you take a pint, you do?' he enquires. One of Mick's greatest pleasures is the pub where, if he chances upon a session, he plays his accordion. He generally heads into Westport or, if a lift is offered, to Aghagower, where he also goes to mass, or over to his father's village of Drummin. 'There was always a couple of old fellows there who'd get steamed up and you would have great craic.' He has cut down his drinking a good deal of late – 'the drink is costly' – and he managed to end thirty years of smoking cigarettes one Lent, just like that.

Mick is a contented bachelor. 'I never bothered my head about marriage,' he says. 'But I tell you, when my father and mother were alive, you couldn't go bringing a woman into an old house like this. And it wasn't easy to put up a new house at that time.' His father passed away in the 1980s at the age of eighty-five. Mick duly took on the farm amid the windswept rolling hills. His older brother had long since decided against the farming life and drove the public bus between Westport and Achill Island for many years.

'I used to grow the best of spuds,' Mick says. 'I often brought a half ton of Kerr's Pink into Westport on a horse and cart.' He stopped growing potatoes in about 1990 and buried the horse five years later. At his peak, he fed and milked fourteen cattle. Today, he has no cattle but keeps a flock of forty sheep, housed in a series of whitewashed buildings behind his house. He makes sure he is out and about on the farm by eight o'clock every morning.

When dusk falls, Mick retires to his living room, an open space lit by a bright, electric strobe light. A Kelvinator fridge purrs in one corner. By and large, he will have a roaring fire in motion, burning turf and whitethorn to create a smell so distinctive of old Ireland that it seeps into your inner soul. His loyal hound, Patch, slumbers on the concrete floor between the fireplace and Mick's armchair.

Mick says this area was considerably livelier in his childhood. 'There were houses everywhere' and people walking on all the roads. 'It's a funny thing,' he muses, 'but when I was a young fellow, lads about twenty or thirty years, I thought they were all old men. They had the big long coat and the hat and it made them all old looking.' The chill winds of the otherworld blow into the room when he talks of those who have died, including many friends who passed this winter just gone. 'I could be alive today and dead tomorrow,' he concludes. 'And isn't it the same for us all? Isn't it equal? I never get the flu. But I'll get something sometime. That's for sure.'

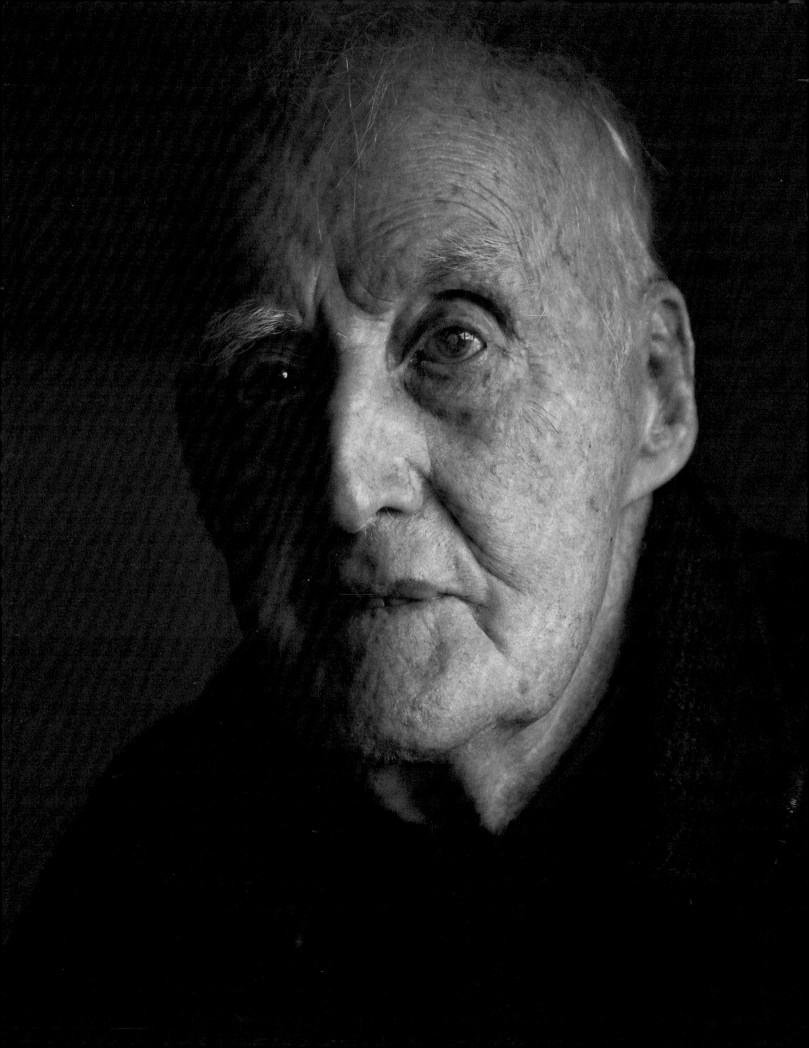

JACK CONNOLLY

Born 1916

Farmer

Glin, County Limerick

'Keep your eyes open, your legs closed and send home your money.' That was the best advice Jack Connolly's four sisters got when they left Ireland in the 1930s, two for the USA and two for England. Emigration was in the blood. Their Uncle Dan became a policeman in New York, and his grandson is still on the beat today. Uncle Jack was due to take on the family farm at Glin but found work on the railroads of Illinois and never returned to Ireland. 'And you know what they say?' says Jack with merry eyes. 'The fool is always left behind.'

Neither Jack nor his father ever left Irish shores. But, as Jack points out, the late Mary Lynch from up the way never even left the parish. And all her family fetched up in America too.

Jack's grandfather, Paddy, moved west from Glenagragra to Glin in the 1860s. He took on the lease of the modest sixteen-acre farm which occupies some of the high ground above the Knight of Glin's demesne. The farm has fine views across the Shannon to the rolling hills of County Clare where Paddy's wife, Margaret McMahon, was born. She had crossed the river to work in Glin Castle as a young girl.

Jack's father, Patsy, worked on the small farm and elsewhere in this landscape of small rush-filled fields, thatched cottages and rickety roads. He drew stones from the quarries for the surrounding roads, did nixers at a nearby blacksmith's forge and became a thatcher of considerable renown. He was very particular about the wheaten straw he used and would not touch straw that had been through a thrasher. 'Broken straw wouldn't last two years,' explains Jack, who was frequently at his father's side, stuffing the rooftops. 'If you did it right and you had a good cut of reed, the roof would last you about ten years.'

Patsy's distaste for threshers may have stemmed from the time his index finger was sliced in two by one. Jack was with him that day and remembers his father washing the severed bone in a stream, wrapping it in a cloth and taking it home. He spent the best part of a month in the Limerick infirmary.

While Patsy earned the money, his wife, Sarah, concentrated on raising their six children, keeping the house in order and milking the cows. She was a Lynch from Ballyculhane and had also grown up on a farm.

In 1918, Sarah went into labour at the thatched farmstead and gave birth to Jack, her sixth and final child. Ireland was in the throes of the deadly Spanish flu which had killed two of Sarah's siblings. The War of

Independence was also close at hand and Glin went through what Jack describes as a 'lively' time. During the Civil War, he recalls how his uncle and first cousin, both IRA members, were obliged to go on the run. Patsy was cutting hay with a scythe when a truck arrived at the farmstead. 'It was the Staters,' says Jack, referring to the army of the Irish Free State. 'They turned the house upside down and pulled everything out, but found nothing.'

Jack went to school in Glin, a half-mile saunter from his home through the Glin estate. It was a doddle compared to the long march his older siblings had to make to their school down in Ballygoughlin. His brother, Mick, was lucky to survive a bout of pneumonia he picked up during one such walk. 'He was crossing a ditch and fell into a dyke. His clothes were drowned but he never told us. They had to get Doctor McDonald down. If a doctor came to you at that time, you were bad.'

Jack secured his first job when, at the age of twelve, he was singled out by the Knight of Glin to carry his bag during a shoot. 'All the lads in Glin had a job carrying the bags for everything they shot and for the cartridges they used,' he explains. 'We got five shillings in the end. It was a fortune. And lemonade.' He was later employed as a beater, charging headlong into deep thickets of laurel, bramble and gorse, urging woodcock and pheasant to fly into the path of the hidden guns. As well as their pay, beaters were rewarded with 'a keg of stout and sandwiches made from real baker's bread'.

During the Emergency, the Glin estate was subject to a Compulsory Tillage Order by which the knight was obliged to convert much of his lawns and his coursing field into barley, oats and potatoes. Jack remembers the knight walking around one rainy afternoon, watching the men at work and muttering, 'They tell you everything about what to sow but they tell you nothing about the damned weather.' Once harvested, Jack helped drive the crop to the pier in Glin from where it would cross the Shannon to the mills of Kilrush.

When he was not working, Jack entertained himself playing football with the lads, walking the land and enjoying the occasional drink. There were plenty of dances in those days, at the hall in Glin, on the pier and, sometimes, 'they had platforms at the crosses [crossroads] where we'd meet on Sunday evenings and it used to be marvellous'.

In 1945, he came across young Mary Culhane of the same parish, to whom he has now been married for fifty-nine years. They have eight children together.

Jack is a quietly lucid individual. He has an encyclopaedic knowledge of family pedigrees in the area. Not only is he able to identify any man or woman down to their nearest (or farthest) second cousin twice removed, but he can reel off the year of their birth, their occupation and their present address. And, of course, he is so venerable that when he talks of Young Bobby Scanlon, it takes a while to work out that 'Young Bobby' is now in his late seventies. Jack may be one of the oldest men in County Limerick, but he boasts a most impressive vigour for life.

PADDY HENEGHAN

Born 1922

Ghillie

Delphi, County Mayo

Through the misty darkness of the night, the figure continued to move slowly towards him. 'I said good night,' repeated Paddy sternly, feeling a cold chill whistle up his spine. The stranger still did not reply. Paddy's right hand clenched at the spade he was holding, the one he had used to help bury his uncle earlier in the day. Why had he not stayed at the wake? he wondered. What was he thinking going up the road at night? 'Whoever you are, you should have spoke!' he shouted. The figure continued to draw near. Paddy raised the spade. 'Good night, Sir?' he roared. The figure hesitated, about-turned and trotted away. 'And what was it?' says Paddy. 'Only an auld skin of a donkey.' Decades after the event, Paddy's relief continues to be immense. 'Only for knowing it was a donkey, I wouldn't be passing on that road ever again.'

You wouldn't have Paddy pegged as an easily intimidated sort. Indeed, he is surely one of the most agile and robust men of his generation. In March 2009, the eighty-six-year-old ghillie helped land the first salmon of the season at Delphi Lodge. We found him by a small, corrugated shed at the back of his house, chopping a fallen alder tree into logs, 'to pass the day'.

Paddy is the third generation of his family to work as Delphi's ghillie. The Heneghans were originally woodmen from Cork. In the early nineteenth century, they came north into Mayo, where they were employed to fell the once-great oak forests that grew along the River Erriff. Paddy has fond memories of his grandfather, Michael Heneghan, who was born and raised near the bridge at Ashleigh Falls. When the 6th Marquess of Sligo took possession of the family fishing lodge at Delphi in the 1890s, he recruited Michael as caretaker of the property.

Delphi Lodge was built in the 1820s by the 2nd Marquess of Sligo, a colourful soul who named it Delphi after a lengthy sojourn in Greece with the opium-toting poet, Lord Byron. Lord Sligo clearly had an eye for location. Delphi is arguably the most spectacular setting in Ireland, with sprightly rainbows and soft mists frequently adding to its Eden-like beauty.

In 1851, Delphi Lodge passed to a Scotsman, Captain William Houstoun, who built a second fishing lodge, Dhulough House, farther north along the shore of Doolough, which is now a crumbling moss-hued ruin, hidden by Scots pines and sprawling rhododendrons. Directly beneath this second lodge is a small

house where Captain Houstoun's coachman once lived and this is the house where Paddy and his two sisters live today. The views from here are as epic as any, with the Sheefry, Mweelrea and Ben Gorm rising steeply on all sides. Paddy has climbed these mountains many times and says he knows every foothold. At the summit of Ben Gorm stand the remains of a shelter built by the Houstouns for lonely night-watchmen. Paddy explains that sheep-rustling was rampant in Mayo at that time. Inevitably, the wind blew the shelter apart but the stones are still there.

Paddy's father, John, moved his wife and their four children to this cottage shortly after he succeeded his father as caretaker of Delphi. Sad times had already befallen the Heneghans with the loss of two children, a baby girl to tuberculosis and a nineteen-year-old boy, described by Paddy as 'the best of us all', to meningitis. Paddy's other brother, Michael, a former ghillie, was the only one to marry and now lives 'at the butt of Croagh Patrick' where he farms sheep.

With so many ghillies in the family, Paddy knew all the secrets to becoming a fish whisperer by the time he was a teenager. He learned the hard way, earning the wrath of his grandfather when, aged seven, he cast his line and caught a pony by the ear. During the 1930s, he and his brothers often walked down to the pebble stone beach that runs along this part of Doolough to fish. Sometimes, the dark waters seemed to shriek, and the Heneghans would think again of the poor souls who drowned near here during a particularly bleak episode of 1847.

On hot summer days, the youngsters swam in the beautiful stretch of the Glenummera River which runs just in front of the cottage. The salmon still spawn in these clear waters but Paddy says the forestry plantations on the surrounding hills have played havoc with the local river system, sending floods gushing out across the road and into a riverside field where his father used to cut hay for the sheep.

During the 1930s, Delphi Lodge was leased to the Fairhursts, a well-to-do family lately returned from British India. In 1936, the family's Scottish chauffeur taught fourteen-year-old Paddy how to drive a car – an invaluable lesson for someone living in such a remote location.

In his late twenties, Paddy tired of life as a ghillie and joined the county council. He slowly worked his way up the road-building hierarchy, crushing stones in the Sheefry Pass in the early days, directing others as he was promoted.

Shortly after, Peter Mantle bought Delphi Lodge in 1986 and reopened it as a fishing lodge. He recruited Paddy as the ghillie. Delphi Lodge remains one of the finest fishing retreats in Ireland and there is a large volume of repeat custom. Paddy still goes out on the water today but 'only with certain people'. There are some, he holds, who 'would take the eye out of you and not notice'.

Paddy keeps himself busy and aims to live long. 'My mother was a couple of weeks short of 102 when she died,' he says with a chin-twitching chuckle. For entertainment, he drives to Leenane twice weekly to pick up his copy of *The Mayo News* and to have a drink in one of the village's two pubs. Paddy complains that it has become very quiet in Leenane lately – he can't remember the last time he heard a good singsong.

Paddy is a happy bachelor. He has loved a few women but never enough to change their name. He recalls one particularly inquisitive neighbour who was forever pestering him about whether he would marry. 'She would nearly want to know what's in your pocket,' he says. 'So I told her I was often married but never churched. And she never asked me anymore.'

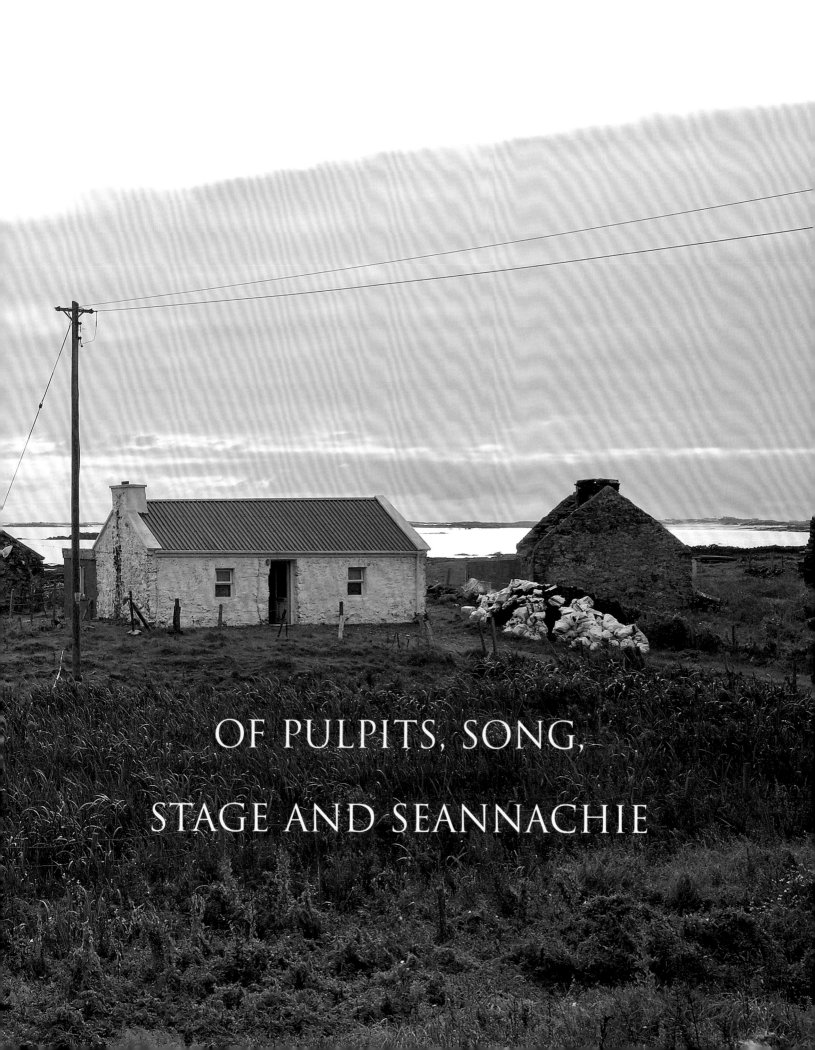

OF PULPITS, SONG,

STAGE AND SEANNACHIE

BETTY SCOTT

Born 1923

Cook and Actress

Rathvilly, County Carlow

Betty's father was out breaking stones for Carlow County Council when she was born in the winter of 1924. As one of thirteen children, William Scott was perhaps immune to the excitement of a new birth. His wife, Elizabeth, was the youngest of seventeen, so she may have empathised with his reluctance to get involved.

William Scott was fifty-one when he married pretty twenty-three-year-old Elizabeth Abbey in Tullow on St Valentines' Day, 1922. The couple broke with their respective family traditions and had just three children. Betty was the eldest, then came Nancy and finally 'sweet little Billy' in early 1930. Photographs of Nancy and Billy adorned the wall of Betty's cottage but their stories are sad ones. William caught pneumonia and died before he reached his teens. Nancy, an aspiring step-dancer, fatally broke her back shortly after her eighteenth birthday.

It is probable that Betty never married simply because she felt so closely bound to her mother. She certainly took it seriously when a travelling gypsy counselled that she would 'never know happiness in marriage'. Betty sometimes wonders whether her life would have been better if she'd found herself a husband, a man who might even have been sitting over in the armchair puffing on his pipe as we spoke. But she didn't find him and that, as she said, was the long and the short of it.

Betty's mother was raised in the convent in Tullow after the premature death of her father. There, she learned enough household tricks to guarantee her work in the Big Houses of Russellstown Park and Duckett's Grove before the First World War. During the War of Independence, she pedalled her bicycle around the county, delivering messages on behalf of the IRA. Kevin Barry, the young Republican student executed by the British in 1920, was one of her neighbours.

In 1937, Betty's mother was employed as housekeeper at Lisnavagh. The new Lady Rathdonnell, matriarch of the house, was a liberal-minded woman. She had lately purged the mansion of its dour and stuffy Protestant staff, replacing them with younger, fresher souls, Catholic and Protestant alike. Betty, at school in nearby Rathmore, helped her mother with the ironing twice a week. On 4 March 1941, Betty started working full time as a parlour maid at Lisnavagh. The war was on and every morning the staff assembled to hear the butler read out the news, transcribed from BBC Radio bulletins. Betty was often entrusted with looking after the Rathdonnell children. A generation later, she was again on hand to help with the children, escorting them to and from the school bus. She worked at Lisnavagh for sixty-four years, becoming the principal cook in the 1960s.

When not working in the Big House, Betty enjoyed sport and drama. In 1948, she collected a clatter of camogie sticks from the Lisnavagh sawmills and distributed them amongst her Ballyhacket team-mates. Clad in white blouses, navy skirts and black stockings, the girls went on to win the Carlow county final that year and Betty has a nine-carat gold medal to prove it.

In 1960, Betty became an active member of Muintir na Tíre, the community development group set up by Canon Hayes in 1937. Rathvilly had a particularly strong community in those times, a fact that helped the small Carlow village win the National Tidy Town competition on three occasions. Betty's focus was theatrical and she was one of the star players of the Rathvilly Drama Group. Indeed, she was voted Best Actress in County Carlow for four years running and won a fifth prize in Dublin. 'I didn't have any lessons,' she says. 'I just learned my lines and that was it.'

The Rathvilly Drama Group travelled around Leinster, performing their plays night after night. 'And the fighting!' exclaims Betty of the behind-the-scenes antics. ' "Fecking auld eejits . . . you don't know nothing . . . you went wrong . . . you can go to hell. . . you done no right." ' She laughs heartily. 'But, of course, I was the biggest devil of them all.'

One of her favourite roles was that of Maggy Butler, the elderly widow who leases Bull McCabe his four acres in John B. Keane's 1965 masterpiece, *The Field*. 'We got a great few awards out of that play,' says Betty wistfully. 'It was the talk of the country. D'you know, I wouldn't mind going again.' Betty abruptly changes her persona. ' "'Tis the field I came to see you about, sorr. My poor husband, God have mercy on him, said – sorr – that if I got into any trouble, I was to come to you." ' Then, almost as suddenly, she metamorphoses into auctioneer Mick Flanagan. ' "Ah, Maggy, you done right to come see me." '

'I was carrying the stick when I played Maggy Butler,' Betty says. 'But I'm carrying it for reality now.' In 2007, Betty's legs seized up with a mystery ailment and she was rushed to hospital. Heavily sedated and on the very brink of death, amputation seemed almost certain. Through the haze, she somehow managed to find a grip. 'It was just a sudden moment,' she says. 'And I thought, Come on, Betty, don't die like this, you know? Don't just die and not make a fight for it.' She attributes her subsequent remarkable recovery to a combination of 'sheer determination on my own part' and the careful attention of the staff of the Hillview Nursing Home where she now resides. 'They have literally bought me back from the dead,' she says. 'Sure I couldn't even put a foot to the ground.'

When Betty walked into the main drawing room at the Hillview for the first time after her legs seized up, all the residents who could stand gave her an ovation and everyone else gave resounding applause. She now walks a little more every day, although her feet are still very tender. They keep her busy in the Hillview, painting, reading and playing bingo. Otherwise, 'I'm just gabbling and giving out as usual,' she says. She misses her old life at Ballybit but, having lived alone since her mother died nearly forty years ago, she concedes that it's good to have some company for a change.

NELLIE KELLY
& CHRISTY KELLY

1922–2007 and 1933–2008

Singer and Musician

Nenagh, County Tipperary

'Two garda up a tree – what are they looking for?'

We met the Kelly siblings in a Day Care Centre in Nenagh in the summer of 2006. Christy was seated on a quilted, two-seater sofa with a box accordion on his knees. His elder sister, Nellie, armed us with tea and currant bread. 'Never mind about the garda,' she said, 'pass the sugar over to the gentleman.' Although the Kellys have sinced passed away they are still held in the highest esteem at the centre, where Nellie was known as 'the resident singer'. She certainly sang with considerable verve for a lady of her diminutive proportions.

'I'm only four foot tall,' Nellie had said to me during our visit, 'but there's good goods in small parcels and when they're lost, they're hard to find.' The mantelpiece in her bedroom was awash with singing trophies and gongs. A photograph of herself and Bertie Ahern held pride of place.

While we drank our tea, Nellie treated us to some of her repertoire, delivering Foster and Allen's finest with a confident, spine-tingling tremble. '"Time from me passes on and I'm growing old, a lifetime nearly gone … but warm is your hand in mine, feeble with ageless time, the light of love still shines, after all these years."'

The Kellys' father was a council worker from Thurles. Their mother worked part time, picking potatoes on farms outside the town during the season. For sixty-four years, the family lived at St Joseph's Park in Nenagh. In 2003, Nellie and Christy moved to a bungalow on Annbrook Heights, which suited them much better as, by then, they both had difficulty walking.

Nellie went to England when she was nineteen and found a job as a housemaid. The future was not particularly wide but at least it was open. Like many of her generation, she never married simply because she felt obliged to look after her own family, particularly when her parents and Christy became ill. She sailed home from England in the early 1950s and didn't leave Nenagh again. 'I never regretted it,' she said. 'I never grumbled and I never answered my mother or father back in my life.'

81

Born in 1933, Christy was the youngest of her four brothers; his twin perished in the cot. He was a well-known character in Nenagh, with his accordion and an enormous arsenal of jokes at the ready. When I prodded him for an answer as to what the garda were looking for in the tree, he replied with comic stoicism, 'The special branch, of course.' He then took up his squeezy box and performed 'Goodbye Johnny Dear'. He maintained that whenever he played the Irish national anthem, his dog would finish the tune with a howl.

In 1938, Christy was involved in an accident that paralysed part of his brain. As he said, 'I took a knock when I was five – it makes me feel giddy.' His words were quiet and humble, almost apologetic.

Nellie treated her kid brother with bossy devotion. While he packed up his squeezy box, she whispered to us, 'He's so good to me! He always has the tea waiting for me when I come home.'

MARY MADDISON

Born 1931

Storyteller

Beara Peninsula, County Cork

'Now, Cessair was Noah's granddaughter,' continues Mary Maddison. 'She was quite a warrior. But Noah wouldn't have her on the Ark so she went off on her own anyway and came on to Ireland and she landed up in Bantry Bay. It's all documented. Her descendents still live in Waterford today, I believe.'

It's probably not a tale she tells every time an audience congregates in her house, but then again, the legends of West Cork and Kerry are one of her storytelling fortes. And that is probably why she has planned for her eventual burial to take place in the pre-Christian churchyard of nearby Kilcatherine, where the petrified remains of the original Hag of Beara are believed to lie.

Mary is determined that the monthly gatherings she hosts are by no means restricted to legends. Indeed, most of the tales spun on those precious Saturday nights are humorous, semi-fictional anecdotes delivered in a rattling poetic language that has to be heard in order for every nuance to be appreciated. 'It's not the story,' says Mary. 'It's the way that you say it. There's humour in everything and we can talk until the cows come home, but it's the old boys that are really funny. The Kerry sheep farmers who come here, the way they tell the stories and the expressions on their faces. When you get into the community here, and you know all the locals, there's a whole different language.'

Perhaps inevitably, the traditions of Irish storytelling survived much longer on the country's offshore islands than anywhere on the mainland. Mary's grandmother was raised on Long Island off the coast of West Cork. Similarly, her mother grew up on Hare Island off Skibbereen, where storytelling traditions were particularly rich. And there were other cousins living in Cape Clear. 'Island people have got a great grá for stories,' explains Mary. 'When you go away somewhere and come back, they'd sit the whole evening and want to know all about it. What did you see? What were the people like? And so on.'

Mary was born and raised in Kinsale, where her father was a shoemaker and her grandfather made boots for the nuns. But all her childhood holidays were spent on Hare Island with her mother's brothers. Day after day, she listened to her uncles talking in a language enriched by the bilingual phraseology of the Irish and English tongues. 'It was sensational,' she says. 'I suppose it's the cells in your body that relate to it but, really, it is a language that you don't forget. If only I'd taped them!' Her uncles also sang, chiefly in the unaccompanied sean nós style with its melodic lilt. 'I could sit and listen to them forever,' says

Mary. One uncle was particularly skilled on the mouth organ and played at all the family's weddings.

When she was sixteen years old, Mary went to England and found work in a hotel in Oxford. One day, she overheard a guest talking about her recent voyages around the world and Mary was suddenly swamped by wanderlust. She took a train to London, went down to the Docks Office and managed to cajole a man there into giving her a job on the *Braemar Castle*, one of the lavender-hulled, Union-Castle liners running between Southampton and Cape Town. The head chef on the ship was an Englishman called Michael John Maddison. 'He was the youngest head chef in the company,' says Mary proudly. 'He had a great sense of humour and everyone used to think he was Irish. We were engaged within six weeks of meeting.'

In the late 1950s, Michael was transferred to another liner while Mary moved to the Cunard liner *Ivernia*, crossing the Atlantic Ocean between Southampton and Montreal. They finally married in 1961 and settled in Hythe outside Southampton, just east of the New Forest. They subsequently moved to the Isle of Wight which, although not quite West Cork, was nonetheless an island. Mary quickly fell into old habits, telling stories to her three daughters at night. 'I never read them books,' she says. 'I just fell into bed and made up a story. It was always something to do with Ireland.' Indeed, even now, whenever Mary goes to visit her grandchildren on the Isle of Wight, she comes back 'absolutely exhausted because I'm up half the night telling stories and reading stones'.

In the early 1990s, the Maddisons bought a site outside Schull and Mary prepared to move back home. However, just as they were about to leave, Michael passed away unexpectedly. When her mourning was done, Mary decided to move farther west to the subtropical Beara Peninsula.

Today, her cheerful home and modest garden look out onto the ocean. Blue mushroom stools are strategically perched between granite boulders. A little donkey and cart rest on a tufted headland. A gaggle of hens, ducks, peacocks and geese amble between a lush, well-stocked greenhouse and a pyramid made of pine. A tiny church, its exterior wall made from seashells, stands beside a wooden shed, which houses what must surely be one of the most impressive shell collections in Ireland.

Mary began collecting seashells when she was a child, building it up during her ocean-faring days. She simultaneously began to gather the beautiful stones that now permeate the rooms of her house. Pots and basins filled with polished amethyst and soothing onyx that pour through your fingers like barley. Crystal bowls that resound with a mesmerising ring and which would be the envy of Angelus stalwarts and Buddhist brass bell-ringers the world over. 'Every stone has a different frequency,' she explains. 'You think you're picking the colour but, in fact, it is the frequency you are sensing.'

Mary is not a woman who will ever be idle. She has a constant stream of visitors, coming to have their stones read or to simply listen to her soothing sing-song voice. She sometimes goes out to sea in her boat; she took up sailing on the Isle of Wight as part of a successful 'life begins at forty' drive. She studies art in Kenmare twice a week and, frequently sits in a small bay window on the first floor of her house, painting the sea and the Skelligs beyond. She frequently contributes to the annual *Eyeries Newsletter* and is presently writing her life history for her grandchildren. And, of course, she hosts her storytelling sessions on the last Saturday of every month. 'When I started, it was just me telling tales. Now we have people from all over coming – Germans, Dutch, French, Polish – and telling stories from their native lands. It's magical really. I have a great life.'

MICK LAVELLE

Born 1930

Entertainer

Westport, County Mayo

The shop bell rings and in strolls Mick Lavelle. He swears he wasn't looking for trouble. He was just looking for some trousers. He'd seen a nice brown pair hanging in the window in Moran's and just happened to walk in as we were asking Dominic Moran if he knew of any old timers in Westport who we should talk to. Dominic laughs like a hyena at the sight of Mick. 'It always happens this way,' sighs Mick. 'I have become well known by accident.'

Mick Lavelle is a singer with a voice that rumbles like brontide thunder. He says his vocals have actually improved considerably since a quadruple bypass in 2006 obliged him to quit smoking. There is also perhaps a more wistful passion in his eyes since the passing of his beloved wife, Annie, in April 2008. Nonetheless, with his eightieth birthday rapidly approaching, there seems to be no let up in this Westport icon.

Mick was elected Culchie of the Year in 1991. He reckons he won the contest simply because he was the only contestant who wasn't flutered on drink. He has been in books and 'on televisions all over the world' ever since. These days, he tends to stay put in Westport. In the evenings, he might spend an hour singing, always unaccompanied, or telling stories and jokes in Matt Molloy's on Bridge Street. In fact, Mick sang with The Chieftains the night the pub opened. His most famous song is probably 'The Millionaire', a raucous ditty about a man who dreams he's won the lottery. He also does a brilliant rendition of Crawford Howard's parody of 'The Green Fields of France'. On other occasions, he might just whistle and lilt. He can even perform a few ditties with his nose.

Mick is known far and wide for his repertoire. He believes he knows the words to over a thousand songs. 'When you're young, there's plenty of room in the old computer but then it gets full up,' he says with a gravelly chuckle. His mind is still full of triggers and if you mention a place like Roscrea or Kildare, he is apt to respond with a verse from 'By the Bright Silvery Light of the Moon' or the opening bars of 'The Roads of Kildare'. And the way he sings the latter instantly catapults your imagination so you're on the roadside where poor Rosie was born. It's a little like hanging out in a musical.

Mick was the fourth of six children, three boys and three girls, born to a couple who farmed sheep in the mountains above Newport. They lived in a thatched cottage and went to school in Skerdagh,

89

surrounded by ruined cabins and blanket bog. His childhood was a hard one 'but people were happier than they are now, anyone will tell you that'. After school, he and his siblings would 'come home and have a bit to eat if they had it'. Then they would head out in their bare feet to gather and spread turf in the bogs. 'Or you'd be put out in the meadows picking stones. You'd come home and wash the feet and into bed and off to school again in the morning.'

Mick says the mountains were a much livelier place to live than the towns in those days. In towns, people went shopping and then went home. In the mountains, people visited one another and stayed a while. 'Ah yes,' says Mick, 'the craic was in the mountains.'

Two pivotal events happened when Mick was sixteen years old. Firstly, his father died of cancer at the age of thirty-nine. Mick watched him go and 'can hear that man roaring yet, no injections, no nothing'. Mick's father was his musical inspiration. 'He'd always be singing the songs when we were kids, when he put us to bed and things,' he explains. Young Mick also collected ballad sheets from an old fellow who would walk around singing particular songs and selling the lyrics on a sheet of paper. 'Music was my first love,' he says. 'It's always kept me going because you meet people and have some craic.'

The second big event of 1946 was that Mick's career as an entertainer began. He had been given the role of a child in a play that was to debut in Dooega on Achill Island. With butterflies running amok in his belly, he drank a pint to boost his pluck. 'I was like the man who was asked why he never got married,' he recalls. 'He was too shy when he was young and he was too old when he got the courage.' Hardly was the drink down the hatch, but Mick was treading the boards and belting out 'The Irish Rover' to a stunned Achill audience. 'At that time, it was all sad songs, you see. 'I'll Take You Home Again, Kathleen' and 'Danny Boy' and all that. But 'The Irish Rover' went down a bomb.' Before long, Mick was performing in houses and pubs from Newport to Glenhest to Burrishoole.

Learning all those songs was fun but spending so much time in the pub had its inevitable conclusions. For starters, he was spending all his money on booze. 'I was out every night, singing songs. I never had enough money to get drunk but people would be buying me drink and then, after a while, they'd say I wasn't capable of singing.' So he quit drinking and, despite spending so many nights in so many pubs, he hasn't touched a drop in fifty years.

When not singing, Mick worked in a welter of jobs – gathering bladder wrack from the shores of Achill Island, tarring the roads of west Mayo, shifting rugs around the Westport Textiles factory, carrying trucks and suitcases around the Railway Hotel. During the early 1960s, he became a porter in Newport House where he met Grace Kelly, Seán Lemass and, most importantly, his late wife, Annie, who was the cook at the time. The Lavelles had no children because Mick was travelling so much in those days.

Mick fears for the future of the quick Irish wit and he is dismayed that so many great songs seem to be disappearing from our collective memory. He holds that young people are too easily ashamed to sing, even though he knows many 'who have lovely voices'. 'Everyone is so busy now,' he says. 'Well, there will be plenty of time when we're dead and gone.' And with that, he disappears into the bar, singing strongly, 'Though time or tide may vary, my heart beats true for thee ...'

VERY REVEREND
PATRICK GILL

Born 1927

Parish Priest

St Patrick's Church, Lecanvey, County Mayo

On 21 September 1795, a group of unarmed Catholics gathered outside Loughgall, County Armagh, to debate ways in which they might resist the recent upsurge in Catholic persecution by the Protestant Peep O' Day Boys. The story runs that this assembly was suddenly attacked by Protestant sharp-shooters and between eight and thirty Catholics were killed, depending on what paper you read. Protestant lore, however, holds that the Catholics attacked first, only to be 'routed with great slaughter by the brave Protestants'. The skirmish became known as the Battle of the Diamond and, that same night, a body of senior Armagh Protestants formally established the Orange Order in Ireland.

Over the ensuing weeks, the order's more thuggish members caused unholy terror to the Catholic population in mid-Ulster, burning their houses, destroying their linen-weaving machinery and driving the families out of the area. 'To Hell or Connaught', Oliver Cromwell's seventeenth-century malediction against Ireland's Catholics, became the Peep O' Day Boys' new slogan. The chilling words were nailed to the front doors of Catholic homesteads across Ulster and prompted a mass exodus.

Among the 7,000 Catholics expelled from Ulster during this period was a barrel-cooper called Augustine Gill, who migrated to the stormy shores of County Mayo. Perhaps, like many Armagh men of that time, he was attracted by the fledgling flax industry on Lord Sligo's estate in Westport.

Four generations later, the legacy of the 1795 pogroms lives on in the memory of Father Patrick Gill. 'When my people arrived here, they were glad to take up a small bit of land anywhere. Even a bit of a bog was better than nothing. They would reclaim it and till it and they grew just one thing – the lumper potato. And when that failed, they were in a bad way.'

Whatever bitterness the Gills felt about being expelled from Armagh mushroomed during the Great Famine, which struck Mayo harder than any other county in Ireland. Father Patrick is of the view that certain landlords in the area were guilty of extracting the maximum from the common people at this time and the Famine is still evidently a very sensitive subject for him.

Born on a farm near Louisburg in 1927, Father Patrick was the only one of his immediate family to enter the Church. His calling was gradual, born during the long periods of prayer time that dominated his youth. By 1945, he was training to be a priest in Maynooth. Having obtained a degree in philosophy and theology, he was appointed parish priest of Mulranny in County Mayo. He was subsequently relocated to Headford in north County Galway. Latterly he was parish priest in the pretty village of Miltown on the upper reaches of the Clare River, between Tuam, County Galway, and Claremorris in County Mayo.

In 1998, Father Patrick retired to the Parochial House of Lecanvey at the foot of Croagh Patrick, just a few miles from the place of his birth. Surrounded by some forty lean young fir trees, the two-storey parochial house was built in the 1920s and overlooks Clew Bay. It stands directly across the road from St Patrick's Church. When Father Patrick's ancestor arrived in Mayo two centuries earlier, the church in Lecanvey was a simple thatched structure set on a small strip of land leased from Lord Sligo. The present, considerable building was completed in 1891 with a modernist porch added in the 1960s. At the back is a community centre where younger folk play indoor soccer, basketball and badminton. The priest is also, of late, the proud caretaker of a FÁS-built polytunnel, pitched behind his house, in which members of the community grow their own vegetables.

On the summit of Croagh Patrick behind the church, you can just see the Oratory where so many barefooted pilgrims find their solace. Father Patrick has climbed the Reek at least twenty-five times and counsels that preparation is key. 'You would want to hone the climbing skills and get a bit of exercise. Oh, boy, does it make the legs sore!'

Father Patrick says he is 'just holding the fort' in Lecanvey, but with 660 parishioners, I sense his retirement is by no means idle. He continues to read, chiefly theology, history and the newspapers. He avoids fiction and has no interest in movies or television. He adores classical music and has even been known to attend the Sunday-night sessions in nearby Stanton's pub. 'Rise up your heart and sing,' he urges. His ambition is to encourage people to be 'kinder, nicer and more compassionate' to one another. He likens the effect to 'a drop of paint in water; the goodness spreads and colours those around about them'.

SISTER ALPHONSUS
& SISTER RITA

Born 1917 and 1920

Nuns

Athy, County Kildare

'And do you not think you'd have had the tea ready, knowing these two were coming?' Sister Alphonsus says, shaking her head testily.

She is, by her own admission, the more commanding of the two. Forty-five years of teaching has instilled in her a no-nonsense outlook on life. But behind the curt words, her eyes roam playfully and she rolls her tongue behind her lower lip, waiting for a reaction.

Sister Rita pays her no heed and continues to lay the table in a calm, gentle manner.

There can be few women who know each other better than Sister Alphonsus and Sister Rita. They have lived together for over seventy years.

It all began shortly before the Second World War when they entered the Sisters of Mercy Convent in Athy, County Kildare.

Sister Rita was the first to join. Her real name is Molly Cranny and she was born in Ballylynan, County Laois, in 1918. Her father, a carpenter, passed away when she was young and the family moved to Athy. In the early 1930s, her elder brother joined the Jesuits but contracted tuberculosis and died when he was nineteen. When Molly came of age in 1938, she, too, chose the spiritual life and entered the Mercy Convent. She took the name Rita after her mother, Marguerite. 'When I went in I was very lonely,' she says, 'and I wanted to come out straightaway.' But she held steady and, in 1941, she made her triennial vows as a Sister of Mercy.

Sister Rita was the youngest of the sixty-five nuns in the convent when Julie Maher, a vigorous young woman from Limerick, entered in 1939. Known as 'Fonzy' by her great-nieces, 'Sister Alphonsus' was born in 1920 to a farming family from the parish of Dún Bleisce on the Tipperary–Limerick border. The community was active during the War of Independence and from the mists of her infancy, she recalls the Black and Tans motoring past their home in a Crossley Tender on the hunt for some rebels who just happened to be her cousins. Julie's father died in 1928, leaving his wife and five small children to run the

farm. 'When we came home from school, you didn't just eat your dinner and sit down,' says Sister Alphonsus. 'There was a good lot of work to be done, milking cows, feeding pigs, picking potatoes off the ridges – big ones for the table, small ones for the pigs. It wasn't hard but it was constant.'

Legend holds that Dún Bleisce means 'the stronghold of immoral women' but all three Maher girls did their best to disprove that theory by joining the Sisters of Mercy. The eldest sister went south to the handsome convent in Skibbereen. When seventeen-year-old Julie voiced her intention of also 'going to Skib', she was advised to go elsewhere or there might be a personality clash. And so she went to Athy. She is not sure what to attribute her calling to save that 'at that hour of your life, you are perhaps not sure what you are doing'. She cannot imagine having taken any other course although she confesses she did have 'a good fling' before she entered. She adopted the name of a priest who helped her by the name of Father Alphonsus.

The nuns slept in double rooms or dormitories and only left the convent to visit sick and bereaved members of the community. 'It was a very sheltered life,' says Sister Rita. 'And it wasn't always easy. But that was the way it was. You did whatever you had to do and there was plenty to be done.'

According to their daily horarium, or timetable, the sisters rose every morning at five forty-five for the Angelus. By the time they sat down for an eight o'clock breakfast of boiled eggs and toast, they had already completed two hours of meditation, mass and prayer time. After breakfast came the 'appointed duties', assigned on a rotation basis by the Reverend Mother. 'Nobody was ever idle,' says Sister Alphonsus, 'and there was a great camaraderie about.'

Sister Rita quickly became a champion of the laundry and kitchen. In the 1960s, she took charge of the House of Mercy, a domestic training school where young girls were instructed in the arts of washing, ironing, knitting, sewing and cooking. She was evidently a fine inspiration because when she celebrated her Diamond Jubilee in 2002, her past pupils organised a large surprise party for her. 'All I could do was break down and cry,' says Sister Rita, who had just returned from burying one of her sisters in England. 'But I enjoyed it afterwards. There was a great turn out, no doubt about it, and they gave me a purse too.'

'And the purse wasn't empty either,' adds Sister Alphonsus.

In 1945, twenty-five-year-old Sister Alphonsus started teaching at Scoil Mhichíl Naofa, where she remained until the school closed nearly half a century later. She has an incredible memory for the names of all those she taught. Indeed, it's easy to imagine that there are women of all ages in Athy whose backs will suddenly straighten on sight of Sister Alphonsus.

The number of novitiates entering the Sisters of Mercy went into decline during the 1950s. Sister Alphonsus believes the slump was inevitable. 'Things got easier for people. There were better opportunities to do things they couldn't do in our time. And there was less of an interest in religion.' Slowly, the sisters' responsibilities were reduced. Both the school and House of Mercy were closed. The convent was sold in May 2000 and the fourteen remaining sisters were relocated. Four went to the hospital at St Vincent's. The other ten, including sisters Rita and Alphonsus, moved into a pair of five-bedroom houses, connected by a conservatory, at Church Crescent on the immediate outskirts of Athy. In 2006, the Convent of Mercy reopened as the four-star Carlton Abbey Hotel.

'I missed it a good deal,' says Sister Rita. 'When we started off here first, we were very lonely. We are farther out of town here so we don't have as many visitors.'

Nonetheless, Church Crescent seems to be a house of much merriment and mutual respect. When Sister Alphonsus regards a photo of her lifelong friend beaming beneath her cap and veil, aged eighteen, she says, 'I wouldn't be living with her for seventy years if she didn't smile like that.' When we suggest photographing Rita in this veil, the sisters break into a loud shriek that has them literally crying with laughter. And when James takes Sister Alphonsus' photo, she wants to know if she can use it on her mortuary card.

A nun's life is a long one. Sisters Rita and Alphonsus are ninety-one and eighty-eight years old respectively. And there are two other sisters in the house who are older than them. 'Life is what you make it, isn't it?' counsels the nun formerly known as Julie Maher.

OF CRAFTS, TRADES,

PUBS AND LABOURERS

ANASTASIA KEALY

Born 1903

Seamstress

Rathdowney, County Laois

Anastasia Kealy is surely one of the only 106-year-olds on this planet still competent enough to live alone. 'Ain't God very good to me?' she marvels. 'That he stayed me alive for so long and I still have my senses?'

It is astounding to think that when Statia's mother, Lizzie Lambert, was born in 1862, Abraham Lincoln was President of the USA and the pedal bicycle had not been invented. In 1880, Lizzie married Tom Kealy, an agricultural labourer from Rathdowney, whose father was a carpenter, coffin-maker and miller. Statia still has a large wooden coal bin that her grandfather made long, long ago. Under Statia's ownership, it has become known as the Magic Box. For men, a bottle of whiskey often seems to levitate from within, while for children there's an infinite supply of sweets.

Tom Kealy worked as a ploughman for the Bartons of Ballinphrase House 'until he got old and got the pension'. In 1897, Tom and Lizzie took the rent on a new two-bedroom stone cottage at Ballinphrase, developed a vegetable garden and gathered some animals – a pig, two goats, a dozen hens, three ducks and a turkey. Statia was born six years later, the ninth of their thirteen children. Infant mortality was high in those times and the Kealys lost six children in a row. 'It was a tough old life,' says Statia. 'But, Lord, I think they were marvellous, the way the poor people lived long ago.' Particularly harrowing was the death of twins born prematurely from shock when Lizzie witnessed Tom slashing his finger on a mower. Statia was old enough to remember seeing her father cycling away with the twins in a hat-box, though she doesn't know where he went. At the time, the Vatican prohibited anyone who had not been baptised from being buried in a graveyard, as they were not yet free from original sin. In pursuit of sacred ground, many parents buried their babies by night in the ring forts scattered around the countryside.

Theirs was a musical household. Her mother played the Jew's harp and mouth organ. Her brother was 'great on the flute'. A sister could play the melodeon. And her father loved to sing. 'And if we had enough of us, they'd play a half-set for the dancing. We were a very happy family, thank God,' she says. Suddenly, Statia breaks into verse.

> *The landlord calls for the rent and I told him no money I had. He said he'd take half, and says*
> *I with a laugh, 'Do you want your old lobby washed down?'*

School was in Galmoy, a two-mile hike across the fields, a journey Lizzie made with her children every day. She always ensured they were presentable, combing Statia's long black curly hair, dressing them up in 'nice white clothes', and 'in summer, she gave us canvas shoes'. Statia claims she was a good pupil and only got 'about two slaps'. 'I was the best in the class to bake a cake,' she says, sounding about a hundred years younger than she is.

After school, the children helped out with chores either on the land or around the house. Sometimes, Lizzie sent them to visit elderly women in the parish, many of whom had lived through the Great Famine. One such woman was Kitty Murphy, for whom they gathered sticks 'for the burning, to boil the kettle'. Kitty rewarded them with bread and butter with sugar on top, and told tales of the 'real hard times, Lord save us'.

One of Statia's first moves when she left school at the age of fourteen was to get her ears pierced. 'I got these little sleepers for five and sixpence,' she says, pointing at her hoops. 'Mammy would give me an egg every morning. So I went without my egg for twelve days and I sold a dozen eggs in town for five and sixpence. I got the sleepers put in my ears and they've been in Statia's ears ever since,' she says with a merry shake of her lobes. Her great-nephew, Father Ian, suggests Statia must be sporting the longest continuously worn pair of earrings on Earth.

Statia has dark memories of the Spanish flu, which killed her cousin's husband the day his daughter was born, and of 'the Black and Tans flying in their big vans'. 'People don't realise what the poor crathurs had to go through long ago. Wasn't it terrible? The way they killed the poor people and put them out of their houses and burned their places?'

Shortly after the Civil War ended, Statia began work as a seamstress in Cullahill for 'a poor invalid on crutches'. 'I was a very good dressmaker,' she says, 'making buttonholes and all like that.'

Statia was the only one of the seven children who did not marry. 'Oh there was a man,' she laughs and then adds rather more seriously, 'but he was a little fond of the glass.' Instead, she devoted her life to looking after her parents. Lizzie Kealy died in 1951 and Tom passed away just over a year later. Statia continued to live at Ballinphrase until she was ninety, when she accepted an invitation from her younger sister, Lizzie, to move to her present home in the shadow of Castledermot's ruined Franciscan abbey.

Statia is pretty sure that times are better today than they were in her childhood but she is puzzled why people seem so dissatisfied. She's full of jovial and slightly racy jokes and loves telling a good yarn. One of her favourites concerns a gymnast of her acquaintance who went into confession. 'Go out and show me how your game works,' the priest said. The young man duly left the box and performed a headstand. Two women waiting for confession looked at each other in shock. 'Oh the curse of God,' said one. 'Look at the penance he's giving today, and I not wearing any knickers.'

Statia is an exceptionally calm individual, completely content on her own or in company. One of her regular visitors is Father Ian, the grandson of her sister Lizzie. The night after Lizzie died in 1994, Father Ian fixed Statia a hot milk with brandy and a spoon of sugar to help her sleep. She had just earned a golden pin for fifty years of service to the Pioneers before he led her astray. Now she has a Baileys or an Irish Mist or a hot milk with brandy every night. Statia Kealy wishes to be waked in the old cottage at Ballinphrase, which was renovated in 1999, and to which Father Ian brings her at least twice a year.

BERNIE DWYER

Born 1936

Butcher

Ballymote, County Sligo

Bernie Dwyer corrugates his brow and regards me with mild dismay.

'She did not "run off" with the tutor,' he corrects. 'She married him. After her husband was dead.'

'She' is Emily, Duchess of Leinster, one of the celebrated Lennox sisters. Between 1748 and 1773, she bore her duke nineteen children and, when the duke perished, she married the tutor – and had another three children. Bernie is correct. He once saw a photograph of the duchess's writing desk with an ingenious curve at its centre, 'designed to accommodate her bump'.

Courteous, eloquent, inquisitive and animated, Bernie is apt to respond with a rising 'go away!' when you gob-smack him with a nugget he did not know before – such as the fact that rugby star Ronan O'Gara, his not-so-distant cousin, was born in California. 'Go away!'

Bernie lives in the building that his grandfather established as a butcher's shop eighty years ago. Retired for many years, this quiet bachelor now spends much of his time seated beside a smouldering fire, reading history books, yellowing newspapers and, his personal favourite, travel articles. He is an enthusiastic explorer and has visited much of Europe, as well as Cairo and the Holy Land.

History has always played a strong role in Bernie's life. His grandmother, who taught him to read in the early 1940s, frequently breathed life into the history books he read by providing a direct link to the events of the past. She was an O'Gara from the shores of Lough Gara at the southern end of the Curlew Mountains. In her childhood, she met many who had lived through the 1836 cholera epidemic, which nearly wiped Sligo off the map, and the Great Famine a decade later.

Bernie's father's family, the Dwyers, were cattle farmers from the musical landscape of Aclare in the west of the county. In the mid-nineteenth century, Patrick Dwyer married Miss Cooke, whose family were prosperous fisher folk, their wealth accrued from the once legendary salmon stock of the River Moy.

Shortly after the Great Famine, Patrick moved his family to the market town of Ballymote and set himself up as a butcher in a single-storey thatched cottage, close to the sturdy rectangular walls of the mighty Norman castle. By the close of the century, his son, Bernard, had converted the premises into a two-storey slated shop with a glass front.

During the War of Independence, Ballymote experienced considerable hardship, much of which stemmed from the shooting of Sergeant Patrick Fallon of the Royal Irish Constabulary in November 1920. Born in Tuam, the redoubtable Fallon had been harassing local IRA members since his arrival in the town four years earlier. He was shot while making his way back to the barracks from the Ballymote Fair. As news of his murder spread, panic erupted across the town and much of the population fled before the inevitable reprisals started. That same evening, six lorries packed with enraged British Auxiliaries motored into Ballymote. Within hours, the town was burning. The creamery, a hay barn, a bakery, a pub and several private houses were destroyed. The *Sligo Champion* reported that but for the exertions of the District Inspector, not a single house would have survived.

Dwyer's butcher shop was not damaged that night. However, the family were propelled into the lime-light when Michael Grey, a first cousin of Bernie's mother, was arrested for Fallon's murder. 'Mick was in the movement all right,' says Bernie, 'but he was not the man who shot Fallon.' Bernie's grandfather, Frances O'Gara, engaged a solicitor for Grey. At his trial in Belfast, Grey repeatedly stated his innocence and many witnesses swore they were with him at the time of the shooting. Nonetheless, he was convicted and sentenced to death. 'And he would have been executed only the Truce came and he was freed,' says Bernie. Grey went on to become a superintendent's clerk in Dublin. The man who did shoot Fallon 'became a bit cracked in later years'. 'He used to go into the pubs and call for two drinks. One for himself and one for Sergeant Fallon.'

In 1927, Bernard's son, Patrick, moved the business up the hill, known as The Rock, to its present location in a handsome, two-storey, mid-Victorian house. Patrick's mother – the former Miss O'Gara – was quick to add her touch, painting the exterior a sky blue and installing finely crafted glazed tiles along the base.

Bernie shows us a photograph from a local newspaper, dated 1942. Entitled 'Tomorrow's Victuallers', it depicts his father standing outside what was then an open-fronted shop, following in the trend of F.X. Buckley's of Moore Street in Dublin. At night, the shop front was secured by high, sliding shutters, although by the 1950s, hygiene laws demanded that all butchers were permanently enclosed.

In Bernie's childhood, his father, uncle and aunt all worked behind the counter. It was a full-time occupation that involved the whole family behind the scenes, including Bernie from an early age. They dealt with all the basic victuals – sheep, cattle, pigs, poultry and rabbits – and slaughtered their own stock. In the 1960s, Bernie's father reluctantly experimented with buying meat directly from an outside supplier. 'It was very good meat,' says Bernie, 'but when the customers knew we weren't killing our own, some of them stopped coming. There's nobody now in the town killing and selling their own stock.'

Today, the shop front is a faded version of what it was in his father's day. The blue paint is peeling fast, the lower door panels are rotting and the fluted timber consoles are crumbling. The old shop itself is now full of late twentieth-century newspapers. 'I intend to read them one day,' says Bernie.

Patrick Dwyer closed the shop in 1976. 'It was his decision,' says Bernie. 'I was sorry it closed but I suppose it was for the best. I was the fourth generation and, at that time, we must have been one of the longest-established businesses in the town.' The knell for Dwyer's was the arrival of several more butchers in Ballymote in the early 1970s. 'They say that competition is the life of trade,' counsels Bernie, 'but competition can sometimes be the death of it too.'

EDWARD HAYES

Born 1924

Houseman and Butler

Kells, County Meath

Edward's life has always been about the Big Houses. They formed the stage upon which his Ireland was set, a time when many of the grand estates were broken up, the houses knocked down, the woodlands felled and the orchards converted to residential estates.

Edward was born outside New Ross, County Wexford, in 1924. He never knew his father, save that 'he existed' and shared his family name of Hayes. His mother, Miss Ellen Cooper, worked as a parlour maid and cook in some of the Big Houses around New Ross. Ellen's father, a slater and amateur stuccadore, was killed some years before Edward's birth and her mother had subsequently married a man named Kehoe (Edward pronounces the name 'Key-ho').

In 1932, Ellen and her young son moved to the Kehoes' small farm of 'fourteen rather bad acres' midway between Carrickbyrne and Ballyshannon. Here, Edward was raised by his mother's three unmarried half-brothers, the Kehoe boys. One operated the knackers' yard for the Wexford Kennels, another was second whip to the Wexford Hunt, while the third worked as an agricultural labourer on a nearby farm.

Edward was fifteen when he left home to work as a yard boy in New Ross. In 1942, he attempted to join the Irish army but was not admitted on account of a chest infection. When he tried to cross the Irish Sea and join the British army, his uncles stopped him. 'What do you want to go and get shot for?' they asked him.

'And so I moved across the water,' he says, 'and by that I mean across the Nore to Inistioge, County Kilkenny.' With its marvellous views and peaceful riverside setting, Inistioge had long been an enclave of the Anglo-Irish gentry. Edward's first job was as a yard boy to the Protestant rector who taught him how to drive.

In 1946, Edward went to work in the yard at Coolmore House, the home of General Solly-Flood, a decorated hero of the First World War. The old warhorse was constantly bombarded with visits from young officers seeking his help with their post-war careers. Many had been in prisoner-of-war and concentration camps.

Sometimes, when extra hands were needed, the butler would summon Edward from the yard to help clear the dining table and bring in the next course. During one Sunday lunch, Edward remembers how the general's wife publicly berated a vicar for failing to visit the sick and needy of the parish. One of the other diners that day was the 6th Lord Teignmouth, who lived nearby, and Edward remembers him looking anxiously at the clock while Mrs Solly-Flood continued her tirade. An enthusiastic supporter of the GAA, his lordship was longing to slip into Thomastown to watch a hurling match. Some years later, Edward came across Lord Teignmouth's diary and found a reference that brought back the memory. 'Lunch Marguerite. Never so bored in all my life. She did nothing but ridicule the Vicar for the entire meal with the houseboy listening.'

Edward maintains that the Second World War had a positive impact on the Anglo-Irish gentry. Many of those he knew closed down their houses during the conflict and went to fight Hitler. When they returned 'they were totally different … they became more down to earth with the people'. By the late 1940s, many of these formerly well-to-do families were facing the fact that their Big Houses were no longer sustainable residences. Edward reels off a list of mansions that were demolished or had their wings clipped.

In the early 1950s, Edward crossed to England, where he spent the summer months working in a bar in Canterbury. During the London Season, he began to chaperone the young Anglo-Irish ladies who were 'coming out' at the innumerable debutante balls and dinner parties. Part of the season involved the presentation of these marriageable young women to the Queen at Buckingham Castle and Edward was on hand to teach the girls 'how to walk backwards, curtsey and not trip up on their dresses'.

In 1957, Edward answered an advertisement in the *Daily Telegraph* and secured a job as a houseman to the Pennefather family of Rathsallagh House on the Kildare–Wicklow border.

For the next four decades, Edward operated as a freelance butler, cleaning, polishing, serving, clearing and babysitting if required. He generally sported a black morning suit or an elegant white smoking jacket given to him by an army man but which later 'fell asunder'. One of his early employers was the artist Pamela

Drew, sometime Lady Rathdonnell, who Edward remembers as 'a woman very much ahead of her time'. She advised him to always be flexible for 'the age of butlers, parlour maids and footmen will soon be at an end'.

Edward moved to his present home in Kells in 1997. He lives in a terraced house, tucked in behind the town centre, with an immaculate front garden. The interior décor is somewhat paradoxical. On one wall there are photographs of the present and previous popes, the Proclamation of Independence and a Sinn Féin flag, with a sketch of Eamon de Valera at its centre, dated 1917. Another wall is covered in postcards depicting stately homes, mostly Irish and all known to Edward, and portrait photographs of the pretty women he once escorted to the London Season. One shelf supports cups and plates emblazoned with royal motifs, such as Charles and Diana's wedding from 1981. A handsome bookcase in the corner is crammed with weighty tomes, such as the well-thumbed copies of *Burke's Landed Gentry of Ireland* and Debrett's *People of Today*. These books provide the names and dates of the cast of characters with whom Edward has worked for the bulk of his life. And he is able to colour in most of those names with gossip of a juicy calibre.

Fans of *Jeeves and Wooster* may recall the code of discretion that exists among butlers. Edward was never an official butler and so his eloquent conversation is liberally peppered with droll tales of the Big House, of foiled thieves, devious daughters, surprise heirs and cantankerous dowagers. Such stories are often accompanied by a heartening chuckle. He seems to know what became of every heir, every housemaid, every hound and every house. 'Such-and-such is owned by a beef baron. That's now a stud. That's a hotel. They burned that one to the ground for the insurance.'

Indeed, while the days of the Big House butler are certainly over, this well-groomed bachelor retains a sound grasp of what is going on, gathered while attending parties and reunions thrown by former colleagues and employers. He sometimes meets faces from the past on his visits to Dublin, browsing in a bookshop or reading newspapers in the Royal Irish Automobile Club on Dawson Street.

EILEEN HALL

Born 1924

Shopkeeper

Killevan, County Monaghan

Miss Hall's shop stands just off the main road between Clones and Newbliss, a couple of hundred metres from the pretty Protestant church of Killevan. It is the solitary shop in the village.

Born in 1924, this amiable spinster has donned her tea-coloured grocer's coat and run the shop for the best part of forty years. The building dates from the 1840s and was originally a straightforward thatched cottage. Her grandfather, Robert Leary, made his money working on farms in Canada. He returned to Monaghan in the early 1890s and established the grocery. A public house once stood next door but its licence was revoked in Mr Leary's day. 'When he died, his son took over,' says Miss Hall. 'Then my uncle, Joseph, had it and, when he passed on in 1970, it came on to me.' Joseph's memory is ingeniously preserved on the exterior of the shop where he trained the climbing ivy hedge to read *J*. Another uncle, Lance Corporal Fraser Leary, served with the Royal Irish Fusiliers in the First World War and was killed in the trenches of the Somme in July 1916.

The timber shelves of Mrs Hall's shop are sparsely bedecked with basic provisions – tea, sugar, bread, cigarettes, peach cocktails, pear halves, baked beans and Brillo pads. In the window, three sun-bleached boxes of Surf washing powder confer beneath a can of fly-spray, a bottle of Dettol and a cylinder of cooking salt. Penny chews and antiquated stationery cling to the old grocery box drawers behind the cash till. A roll of postage stamps lies upon the countertop. To her right is a small cast-iron fireplace, turf burning to keep her warm, a rarity in any shop in twenty-first-century Ireland. Other than the fire and a single, bald, overhead bulb, the room is illuminated by the daylight that comes through the sash windows. Monaghan tends to be a rather dark county, so it is as well Miss Hall has the light-bulb.

It was not so long ago that all lamps in these parts were paraffin based. Certainly, paraffin was one of the shop's big sellers in the 1940s and 1950s. The arrival of 'the electric' put paid to that, says Eileen, but it was not without controversy. Many of the older generation believed electricity was the devil's work and refused to have it in their houses.

Classic advertising posters adorn the walls. 'Insist on Sunlight – So Kind to Clothes and Hands'. 'Look Your Loveliest with Luxurious Nightcastle'. 'Chesterfield Cigarettes' and 'Wills Woodbines' tobacco.

Eileen used to stock plug tobacco but gave up when she realised that nobody in the parish smoked a pipe anymore.

In 1845, the *Parliamentary Gazetteer* estimated that the parish of Killevan comprised 4,933 Roman Catholics, 1,820 'Churchmen' (i.e. Protestants) and 520 Presbyterians. 'There used to be a lot more houses here one time, all thatched,' confirms Eileen. 'It was a much bigger community. But they were all tossed down, a hundred at one time. There wouldn't even be fifty people here now.' Part of the problem was the decline of this part of the country generally. The Troubles were partially to blame but the closure of the railway line from Newbliss and Clones was also a terrible blow.

Rural shops like Miss Hall's will not survive for long. There is simply too much stacked against them. The most obvious predators are the supermarket and the garage shop. 'They have taken away from the small shops,' says Eileen. 'They have more variety and it's very difficult to compete on price.'

Most of the time, it is so quiet in Killevan that all you can hear are the rooks rustling in the treetops and the bubbling waters of the River Finn pouring over the rocks nearby. But the peace of Miss Hall's shop is frequently decimated by the racket of the boy racers who zoom up and down the road beside her in the summer evenings and at weekends. She believes the lack of discipline in the younger generations is the fault of their parents. 'They're too busy working,' she says. Conversely, these young men clearly have 'too much time on their hands'.

CEADÚNUITHE
CHUN
STAMPAI
DO DHÍOL

LICENSED
TO SELL
STAMPS

MURRAY'S
'WARRIOR'
PLUG
TOBACCO

WARRIOR PLUG

"NUGGET"

REGISTERED TRADE MARK

BLACK

WATERPROOF · FREE FROM ACID
THE FINEST
BOOT POLISH

Puss reflects on Nugget quality

WILL'S
WOODBINES

10 FOR 4D
15 FOR 6D

FRANCIE McFADDEN

Born 1929

Gravedigger

Carrigans Upper, County Sligo

Glancing out his bedroom window on the evening of Monday, 24 February 1947, seventeen-year-old Francie McFadden shivered. The penetrating Arctic winds had been blowing for several weeks and, that night, the first powdery flakes began to fall. By the morning, the world – or Ireland at least – was utterly unrecognisable. Every field, road and rooftop was submerged under a thick blanket of snow. Known to posterity as 'The Big Snow' or 'The Blizzard', this was the greatest snowfall of the twentieth century and lasted nearly forty-eight hours until midday on Wednesday. The freezing temperatures solidified the snow's surface and it was to be a biblical forty days before it began to melt.

'People said Ireland was finished,' says Francie. 'It was pure black frost, night and day constant, and the snow was as high as the hedges. A lot of the houses around here were backed up to the roof.' For old-timers, those bone-chilling weeks marked a dreadful era and many succumbed to the temperatures. Amongst the dead were two colleagues of Francie's father who were caught in a snowdrift while returning from the bogs. They were found four days later with the bags of turf frozen on their backs.

But it was also a time of collaboration and resourcefulness. Francie recalls how the quick-thinking bakers and milkmen of Sligo constructed sleighs from old barn doors and attached them to their donkeys and horses in order to supply their snow-besieged customers. Similar sleighs were used to carry coffins, although sometimes it was easier to find six men to carry the coffins up the railway tracks.

For the younger generation, however, the snow provided much entertainment. When the seventeen springs of Bellinascarrow Lake were found to have frozen to a depth of nine feet, a group of young lads took the shoes off their horses, loaded their carts up with several tons of sawdust from the Ballymote mills and poured it all over the icy surface. 'And didn't they set up a stage on the lake with poles and lights and big heavy batteries!' marvels Francie. 'They had bands and done dancing on it and the music could be heard above Boyle.' One foolhardy gent won a whopping thirty pounds when he drove across the lake on a BSA motorbike.

Francie's father was one of twelve children. Francie was one of twelve children. And Francie is the father of twelve children. All thirty-six McFaddens were born and reared in the house where Francie lives today.

In a field just opposite the McFaddens stands a megalithic boulder with the ghostly profile of a man carved on one side. Archaeologists have discovered the tracts of thirty-seven small but distinct houses in this same field. 'Every house had one room and a kitchen and maybe enough land to keep a goat,' says Francie. The ancientness fascinates him, and he has a healthy respect for the spiritual. He points to an ash tree growing close to a nearby holy well and tells us of a local farmer who became obsessed with the idea of burning it, but despite all his endeavours – which included surrounding the trunk with burning coals – the ash has survived while the farmer is long dead. 'Never harm a holy tree,' warns Francie. He recalls an old lady, born in the Famine, who used to come out to the same tree, brush its trunk with lime and fix ribbons to its branches. A swing used to hang from one of its sturdier limbs, though Francie confesses that nobody ever swung with complete confidence, as one slip might leave you face down at the bottom of the well.

Francie's great-grandfather 'Old John' McFadden was a blacksmith. His father Frank made his money cutting turf on the bogs a mile or so from Carrigans. The bog is also where young Francie earned his first shillings, heading out with a donkey and cart, day after day, gathering, shaping, drying and distributing. He has a special fondness for the place. 'It was like the seaside,' he insists. 'And it was very healthy work.' When he was not working the bog, Francie was out with a scythe, mowing pastures and hedges on Frank Oliver's 150-acre farm for one pound a week. 'That was enough to get a few pints,' he says.

Local legend has it that Francie could put away thirty pints a day in his prime but he is not easily drawn on the subject. 'A few will do you no harm when you're working,' he advises. 'And working will do you no harm, as long as you don't overdo it.'

Francie was a keen fisherman in his younger days and still revels in a huge pike – 'by god he was a monster' – he caught with his brother and another man by the bridge in Temple House Lake. He also played accordion with a band in Castlebaldwin on Sunday nights.

When the Second World War ended, Francie moved to England and found work on the building sites of Luton and London, where he narrowly avoided death. 'I was up high, wheeling concrete along a plank and didn't the plank crack. There were six men under me. I was lucky at the sort of timber in the plank. It didn't crack on the snap. It backed up for me. Nice and slowly. A cool head and dry feet were needed. If I'd gone over, the men below would have been killed by the concrete, and I along with them. When I came down the ganger said, "Were you ever in the circus?" "No," I said, "but I've met an awful lot of hooring clowns."' The incident didn't deter him from heights but he always checked the quality of the timber ever after. 'I often heard jockeys say that if you fall off a horse, you have to get back on straightaway or you will lose confidence.'

In the early 1960s, Francie returned to Ireland, where his digging skills earned him a full-time job as a gravedigger based at Carrownanty Cemetery in Ballymote, though he worked at graveyards all around the county. He's not sure how many graves he has dug since, but 'the Lord save us, there must be hundreds and hundreds'. In the old days, he travelled about on a Honda 50 with a shovel, pickaxe and fourteen-pound sledge strapped to the side. These days, the eighty-year-old widower journeys to the graveyards by tractor and, despite his great age, 'I still dig them yet'.

GRETTA CARTER

Born 1921

Lacemaker

Borris, County Carlow

At 6:45 a.m. on 3 January 1941, the people of Borris woke to a very loud bang. A German bomber flying over Ireland had dropped its bombs along the Carlow side of Mount Leinster. Struggling to maintain altitude, the pilot had apparently offloaded them to reduce the plane's weight. One stick of eight bombs exploded on a house at Knockroe, killing three women. As news of the tragedy spread, a team of first aid trainees from Borris raced up to Knockroe to look after the wounded. Among the trainees was twenty-year-old Gretta Knipe, who fainted when she arrived.

Gretta was the only child of Felix Knipe, the bailiff of Borris House, which was the home to the MacMurrough Kavanaghs, the ancestral kings of Leinster. As the church organist, Felix was a well-known figure in the village. He was also one of the mainstays of the Borris Brass Band and played in goal for the Borris Gaelic football team. His father, Arthur Knipe, moved to Borris from County Antrim to serve as a sergeant in the Royal Irish Constabulary during the late nineteenth century.

Gretta's mother also worked in Borris House but died as a result of childbirth when Gretta was only three days old. Gretta was then reared by her aunt, May King, the supervisor of Borris Lace. Lady Harriet Kavanagh had first established the lace-making industry in Borris during the 1850s. She had brought back lace patterns from Italy, which she had modified before personally teaching the women of the village how to copy them. Every week she distributed work to women from the poorest families, thus enabling them to add to the paltry wages of their menfolk. Aided by the Kavanaghs' international contacts, Borris Lace rapidly became famous for its beautiful, intricate patterns, finding its way to stately homes as far away as Russia.

While her husband was at work, Gretta kept herself busy, helping Aunt May with the lace. By the 1950s, however, there were only six women employed in the industry. The lace patterns were simply proving too costly to sustain the business. Gretta watched her aunt braiding and laundering all the collars, doilies and tablemats, and learned how to stitch. Although she was never a professional, Gretta made enough of these exceptionally complex laceworks to ensure that, today, she is known as the last of the Borris lace-makers. Arguably her finest moment came when the Irish Countrywoman's Association asked her to present a lace tablecloth to Mary Martin, the American musical actress and mother of *Dallas* star Larry Hagman.

A year after the Knockroe tragedy, Gretta married Paddy Carter. He, too, was an only child and his father was a soldier in the British army. Paddy was an odd-job man who worked primarily as a yardman for Cody's of Borris, but later he became an insurance agent with the New Ireland Insurance Company. In 1944, their daughter, Esther, was born, followed by three sons.

Gretta Carter belongs to a generation who always kept their door open and the kettle on the boil lest a passer-by be thirsty for a mug of tea. Although her eyesight has failed in recent months, her memory will always recall an age when the best remedy for the common cold was a pinch of snuff. She now resides at Borris Lodge Nursing Home.

JAMES McGARVEY

Born 1942

Labourer

Clones, County Monaghan

James McGarvey is one of the best-known faces in the border town of Clones. He can often be spotted making his way down Fermanagh Street, ambling across the Diamond or talking with friends in the shadow of the ancient Round Tower. When not in public view, he is almost certainly in a public house. The joys of celibacy mean James has little to trouble him other than raising the price of a pint.

His father, Mick McGarvey, was a thatcher and grew up on a farm at Lisnagore, a few miles west of Newbliss. 'Daddy thatched every house in the county,' says James. 'And at that time every place outside Clones had a thatched roof.' In 1920, Mick married Rosie Smith, a farmer's daughter from across the border in Roslea, County Fermanagh. 'I don't know how they met but they come together anyway and I'm the living proof of that.'

James was the sixth of Mick and Rosie's nine children. He had a nomadic boyhood, fetching up on a small farm by Newbliss, with a goat and 'a lock of hens'. The young McGarveys were educated at the Largy School on the Analore Road outside Clones. James says he was 'kept back so long at the Largy' that, by the time he left, all the other kids thought he was the teacher.

When his schooldays were finished, James took on work as a seasonal labourer, shovelling, fencing, threshing, building the roads. In the evenings, he went 'night-fishing' with tilly-lamps, casting for perch in the winding waters of the River Finn.

During the early 1950s, Clones was one of the busiest towns in Ulster. It was a major Great Northern Railway (Ireland) junction, where the routes from Enniskillen, Armagh, Cavan and Dundalk converged. The streets were lined with buoyant shops and its pubs were esteemed for the high calibre of their traditional music. James and his older brother, Johnny, frequently herded cattle into Clones for the Thursday markets. 'There'd be nothing only cattle in town and the place would be packed.'

James McGarvey's accent carries the unmistakable nuances of an Irishman who has worked for many long decades in England. It is not always easy to understand him. He speaks in riddles, cracks jokes from the sidelines and cackles harmlessly at the world going by. But between the jigs, he explains how he left Ireland in 1957, the year the Clones railway station was shut. 'I was only a wee lad of fourteen and a half when I went but I built the British Rail,' he says. 'A man called Paddy McManus, a ganger on the railway, sorted me out. He said, "Come on out", so I did. I waited a couple of days and he got me the job. Whenever I left this country, I was getting three pounds and ten shillings a week. When I went there, I had to work a fortnight, but when I did get paid, it was big stuff!'

James's first big job was to remove all the old tracks and lay down new ones between Huntington and Peterborough. Relaying this information, he casually asides that Oliver Cromwell came from Huntington and that Catherine of Aragon is buried in Peterborough. Clearly those extra terms at the Largy did him some good. When not working on the railways, he was employed at the Shell Haven oil refinery on the north bank of the Thames. He stayed in England for 'thirty years all up' and maintains that he never encountered any of the 'No Irish Need Apply' attitude. On the contrary, he worked 'with some of the finest English fellows you'd ever meet in your life, damned good lads they were'. He finally returned to Ireland in 1987, got a job with Monaghan County Council and settled in a house between Clones and Cootehill.

Music has never been far away. 'Daddy could play the bow-fiddle and the accordion,' says James, 'and I sang the odd time.' One of his father's favourite venues was Treanor's Bar on Fermanagh Street where he often played with Tom McGeough from 'up the mountain'. Treanor's remains one of James's preferred taverns today, although he and his brother, Johnny, might also be found supping brandy and stout in The White Star or The Towers. The brothers know the pedigree and lineage of every pub in town, the name of every landlord who ever owned it and possibly the date of its establishment. 'I don't think I will marry now,' says James. 'Not the way things are going. But what can you do though? All you can do is the best you can.'

JIM KIELTY

Born 1917

Hackney Driver

Ballymote, County Sligo

'Gentleman Jim' Kielty reckons he has clocked over 2 million accident-free miles during his eighty years behind the wheel. It began in the summer of 1932 when, aged fifteen, this publican's son from Ballymote took the wheel of his father's Model A Ford for the first time. 'Cars have always been my passion,' he explains. His father owned one of the very first Model T Fords in the town, a sturdy 'Tin Lizzie' built in 1916. 'TGI 709,' says Jim, emphasising each letter and digit of the car's registration with pride.

During the War of Independence, the IRA commandeered the family car. Indeed, Jim's father, James, regularly drove Countess Markiewicz to political rallies in the county. They were often accompanied by a plucky young woman from Ballymote, Miss Baby Bohan, nicknamed 'The Green Countess'. Countess Markiewicz's brother, Sir Josslyn Gore-Booth, owned most of Ballymote, though his aristocratic credentials did not stop British Auxiliaries setting fire to the town in 1920 in reprisal for the murder of Sergeant Fallon.

'This was always a tough town,' says Jim. One of his earliest memories is of General Farrelly's Free State troops storming the barracks at Ballymote in July 1922, when they captured the garrison of Irregulars within. 'The things that man can remember,' laughs his wife, Catherine. 'I'd say he could remember being born.'

Jim was born in the family pub on O'Connell Street in 1917. When his father first took on the pub in 1901 (after abandoning a career in insurance), Ballymote had a population of just 997 people and had twenty-seven pubs. Kielty's pub was popular with war veterans. 'I heard a few traumatic stories about Gallipoli and the Dardanelles,' recalls Jim. 'Some of the men were badly scarred and that left quite an impression on me.' One local legend was Martin Moffat, a private with the Leinster Regiment, who won the Victoria Cross when he single-handedly killed two Germans and captured another thirty in Belgium in 1918.

Like most of the town's children, Jim was educated in the local National School, close to Ballymote Castle, the magnificent fortress built by the powerful Red Earl of Ulster, Richard de Burgh, in 1300. The ruined Franciscan foundation nearby was once a celebrated seat of learning. Its resident monks penned an epic collection of historical, genealogical and romantic writings during the fourteenth century, known as the Book of Ballymote, which is now in the possession of the Royal Irish Academy.

During Jim's childhood, O'Connell Street was a sandy track, full of horses and carts laden with turf. 'We used to look forward to the big fairs when all the farmers came in to town to sell their animals. The street was literally black with cattle at times.' He has fond memories of playing in the corn mills and bleaching greens of the Keenaghan mills with their Alpine-style pylons. 'They closed down in 1940 on account of the war as there was no Indian corn coming in.' In October 1941, the mills caught fire and burned to the ground although their ruins can still be seen today.

Jim remembers his father being kitted out for a game of football with the Round Towers, the local team who met on Davey's Field beneath Carrownanty Hill. The team was named after a thirty-foot-high obelisk built on the hill's summit by Lady Arabella Denny, founder of the Magdalen Asylum and an aunt of Lord Shelburne, the eighteenth-century British prime minister. When the rent was due from Lady Arabella's many tenants, a white flag was hoisted high upon the tower, visible for miles around. During the 1970s, diggers quarrying sand from Carrownanty Hill undermined the tower's foundations and down it fell. The Round Towers team peaked in 1938 when they reached the FAI Junior Cup quarter-final but lost 6–5 to Killybegs. In time, Davey's Field was incorporated into the ever-expanding Ballymote cemetery.

In 1932, while Ireland geared up to host the Eucharistic Congress, Jim obtained his driving licence and started work as a hackney driver. His first job was to meet a funeral coming from Carrick-on-Shannon. He drove an Austin 19-6 and, later, a gleaming Austin Cambridge ('a very strong model and ideally suited for hackney work'). He kept the bills down by doing his own repairs, but even then the price of petrol stung. 'The Austins were built like tanks, but you would need a tank coming behind to keep them filled up.'

O'Connell Street, Ballymote.

'Fair Day was very busy for us,' he says. 'And I used to deliver barrels of beer out to country house weddings and wakes all over the county.' His longest journey was to Cork city and back in one day, a round trip of 420 miles. And arguably his closest escape was during The Big Snow in 1947 when he narrowly made it home to Ballymote from Dublin before the roads became impassable. 'It was hard to get a few bob then, so you'd do all the hours you could.'

Although the sound of stout being tapped in the barrels echoes through his childhood memories, life as a barman never really appealed to Jim. 'I just didn't like it,' he admits. 'There was nothing to it.' In 1960, he shut down the pub. Six years later, eager to spend more time with his family, the fifty-year-old quit the hackney game and began a sixteen-year stint driving buses for CIÉ for 'the school run and local journeys'.

In 1951, Jim met Miss Catherine Hopkins, a farmer's daughter from Baltinglass, County Wicklow. 'I got a fishing hook onto her and got her up here,' he says. The couple had a son, who died of cystic fibrosis, and four daughters, three of whom are now teachers.

'Gentleman Jim' takes a drive back in time

DRIVING SEAT: James Kielty in a

MANY IRISH towns have walking encyclopae-dias.

But it's doubtful if many town have a driver/historian who has clocked up 2.5 million miles and never had an accident.

And gentleman James Kielty has been driving since 1932 - the year of the Eucharistic Congress, and also the year he got his very first driving licence.

However James Kielty is still driving at the age of eighty-five.

Cars of all shapes and sizes have been an abiding passion for a Ballymote citizen whose father drove the late Countess Markievicz and who can remember Ballymote barracks being burned in 1921.

James Kielty's earlier youth was full of Model T Fords, Austins and country trips bringing barrels or porter to country wakes and weddings.

It's a vanished world but one that James recalls with photo-graphic precision.

'I grew up in a pub in Ballymote in O'Connell Street and there were twenty seven pubs in the town in those early years.

And James has a meticulous record of all the pub owners up to the present day.

'I was born in 1916 and one of my earliest memories is of see-ing the stout being tapped in the beer barrels in our pub.

'At that time there was no draught and you had to tap the stout before consumption.

'I also remember my father telling me that he drove Countess Markievicz in his

ABOUT THE WRITER

Swirling tales of scarred World War One veterans, gleaming Austin cars and Ballymote in the 1920's are just some of the highlights of the eclectic career of eighty-five-year-old James Kielty who has driven 2.5 million miles and never had an accident.

Model T Ford car and I also vaguely recall Ballymote bar-racks being burned in the early 1920's.

'Ballymote was a very differ-ent place in those days.

'We used to look forward to the big cattle fairs when all the farmers came in to town to sell their animals.

'The street was literally black with cattle at times.

'Fair Day was a very busy day for us and we also used to deliv-er barrels of beer out to coun-try house weddings and wakes.

'Ballymote had a number of soldiers who fought in the Boer war and in World War One.

'And I remember some of them coming and telling us traumatic stories about Galipoli and the Dardanelles.

'Some of them were badly scarred and that left quite an impression on me.

'I drove my first car in 1932 after getting my driving licence at fifteen.

'It was my father's 14.9 Ford and I went to meet a funeral coming from Carrick-on-Shannon.

'That was the start of fifty happy years in the hackney business where I drove some famous people from all over the North-West.

'I even drove at a couple of elections but I gave that up as it proved costly.

James' customers included commercial travellers, politi-cians, doctors and distin-guished visitors to the town of the Red Earl William De Burgo whose castle is a reminder of Ballymote's Norman past.

'Cars have always been my passion and I did all my own repair work on all the Fords and Austins I had on the road.

'The cars in those days were built like tanks but you would need a tank coming behind them to keep them filled with petrol.

'But there wasn't as much

traffic on the roads in those days either.

'Circuses were very popular in those days and one particu-lar artist used to come out of a coffin as part of his act.

'I was transporting the coffin for him in the back of the car one dark night when it slipped off and I on my way to Tubbercurry.

'I heard afterwards that a passer-by took off like a rocket after he saw this coffin sitting at the side of the road.

'But the coffin was retrieved and delivered safely.

'I also used to bring barrels of stout out to country weddings and wakes.

'Those were big occasions in the 1930's and 40's.

'Cars were much cheaper in those days also and you would pay £250 for a new Austin car in 1949.

'I continued to drive all through the fifties, sixties and seventies when I finished up with an Austin Cambridge car.

'The Austin Cambridge was a very strong model and ideally suited for hackney work.

'But even though he has reached four score and five, Jim Kielty still drives.

'I am a relief driver these days for various people and I still enjoy it.

'But I am still very interested in the history of Ballymote which has a fascinating past.

But a large part of that histo-ry would include its own gentle-man Jim who is certainly a walking encyclopaedia of Ballymote in the twentieth cen-tury. Maybe he should start his memoirs.

JOAN CROWLEY

Born 1922

Publican and Fiddler

Kenmare, County Kerry

Crowley's Bar on Kenmare's Henry Street is considered one of the finest traditional pubs in the Kingdom of Kerry. It was a vital sanctuary for Irish music when that genre became endangered in the 1960s and 1970s. 'We were the first that I remember to have traditional music here,' says Mrs Crowley, who ran the bar for many decades with her late husband, Con. 'It used to be that nearly every house in the town was a pub then, but they didn't have music. It wasn't allowed in the old days. They didn't want people singing in the pubs.' But when rock 'n' roll and 'loud pop music' began seducing the youth of Kerry, the Crowleys were to the fore in the promotion of traditional music. It wasn't all about the music, mind you. 'I thought it was a great help for the business and it was a fine attraction for tourists.'

By the 1980s, men and women were coming in from miles around to 'sing songs and play a few tunes' on Crowley's chairs and stools. 'They were real musicians – they'd hear a tune and pick it up.' A fiddle was kept behind the bar for anyone who wanted to have a go. And, if you were lucky, you might even hear the Crowleys play. Con Crowley was highly accomplished on the accordion and his wife was as nimble as an eel on the fiddle.

'I haven't opened it for a long time,' she says, fiddling with the clasps that hold her fiddle in its case. On account of two arthritic fingers, she laid her fiddle down some years ago, but the all-powerful omega oils have been at work on her bones and now her fingers reach out for the bow. 'I'm not a traditional musician at all,' she laughs. 'I was taught how to read it.' In the early days, she and Con often practised together at home. That became trickier with the pub, as one or other of them would always be working behind the bar. But some nights, the Crowleys would play to the crowd. They followed the graceful Sliabh Luachra style, popularised by Kerry fiddlers such as Julia Clifford, her brother, Denis Murphy, and the mighty fiddle-master, Padraig O'Keefe.

Joan Crowley was born in Kenmare in March 1922. Her only sister, Mary, was born nearly three years earlier in Boston. Their father, Tom Lovett, was raised on a mountain farm at Gortnaboul, near Kenmare, but emigrated to America on the eve of the First World War. He found work as a janitor in Boston and found a wife in Mary O'Connor, a farmer's daughter from Killorglin in north Kerry. In 1921, when Mary was pregnant with Joan, the Crowleys sailed back across the Atlantic and began farming in Templenoe.

Young Joan walked to the school in Templenoe until she was eight years old. She then headed into Kenmare to spend close on a decade at the Poor Clare Sisters' convent, once famous for its Kenmare Lace. At the age of eighteen, she tried to get a job in the civil service and fetched up as the accountant in Halissey's General Store on the Square. Meanwhile, her sister, Mary, married upholsterer Bill Brannigan and settled in Dublin's Artane, where they raised five children. Joan still sees her sister regularly. 'She comes down a bit and I go up. She's older than I am and she's able to drive a car.'

Joan stayed at Halissey's, totting up the figures, until her first child was born. 'Married women weren't encouraged to work at that time,' she explains. 'You were expected to stay at home.' To look at Mrs Crowley, you could not imagine that this slight, self-effacing, defiantly girlish octogenarian has raised a dozen children. But when she pulls the photograph down from the sill and names each child, there can be no doubting she's their mother. Joan was 'just twenty-two' when she met Con Crowley and 'nearly twenty-three' when she married him. It was January 1945, and the war was still raging in Europe. She talks a little of each child and explains how two of her daughters have passed away, one from cancer, the other from a fall. 'So that's two of them gone – but the rest of them are all here.' The hurting briefly fills the room but she's quick to rise to it.

Understandably, she has lost count of her grandchildren. She does her best to remember their names. 'In my day, everyone was called Paddy or Dan or Mick. Now my grandchildren have names like Enda and Mark and Ross and names you never heard of.'

Today, Mrs Crowley lives in a simple terraced house between Kenmare's main square and the pretty Finnighy River that runs through the town. Pope Benedict and St Charles of Mount Argus gaze benevolently from the mantelpiece. Mrs Crowley often sits by the stove, talking with visitors and reading novels from her well-stocked bookcase. The living space is all open-plan and big windows to compensate for all the time she spent in the cramped confines of the pub. 'I was indoors most of my life because of the bar. You don't get the sun, and it's the sun what gives the farmers the country look.'

Mrs Crowley's son, Peter, who now owns and runs the bar, maintains its musical theme by hosting sessions on Monday and Tuesday evenings, with impromptu sessions apt to kick off any other night of the week.

JOE McCABE
& MICKY LALOR

Born 1919 and 1931

The Hurler and the Water Diviner

Abbeyleix, County Laois

Micky Lalor is anxious to set the record straight. His daughter is married to Joe McCabe's son. And Joe's father was Micky's schoolteacher in Clonad. And yes, okay, Joe's father did have a wee romance with Micky's mother. But that was a long time ago, before anyone was married. Above all, he and Joe are neighbours – and always have been.

It is clear that Joe and Micky regard the ongoing link between their two families as a happy coincidence. They are great pals. Joe swears Micky is 'one of the best water diviners in Ireland – bar none'. Micky says Joe's record as a hurler speaks for itself. The two were taking afternoon tea and cream buns when we called in to the McCabe house in Ballyroan outside Abbeyleix on a wet spring afternoon.

They sat in opposing armchairs, chuckling at the old times, at stories they've heard a hundred times before. There is the story of the kindly fool who accidentally donated the entrance fee for a vital hurling match to the parish priest. Or the scoundrel who had the monopoly on bicycle tyres and wireless batteries during the war. Or the hurler who kept all his money in a matchbox but accidentally lost the box while making haycocks 'so he had to unravel all his cocks with a pitchfork and start over again'. And what of Jack Lyons, a big lad who had to get a bypass? 'Doctor, a bypass is no good to me – I need a roundabout.'

Joe is the first of his McCabe line for four generations to not become a teacher. 'I have sisters who were teachers. I have a daughter teaching – and a grandchild teaching too! But teaching was not for me!'

Instead, he evolved a passion for hurling. As a child, his native county still echoed with the roars of those who had carried Laois to victory in the 1915 All-Ireland Hurling Championship. The weather had been so wet that day that the two teams played the second half in overcoats. One of his many colourful tales involves a midnight raid on a prosperous farm to pinch a lump of ash to make some new hurls. Luckily, even at the age of twelve, Joe could run.

In the GAA's Jubilee Year of 1934, the fifteen-year-old Joe McCabe, clad in short trousers, played for the Laois Minors in a match that saw them become Leinster Champions. Next up was Tipperary in the All-Ireland minor final at Croke Park. What an astonishing prospect for any fifteen-year-old.

'None of us knew Dublin,' he says of his team-mates. 'We arrived with nothing only our boots, tied together and thrown across our backs. And we carried our hurls in our hand. We had no cases, no pyjamas or anything at all. We walked along the quays and then up to Barry's Hotel. We went to the pictures that night. The Plaza! I remember it was four old pence. We came out of it after and there was a chipper. We never had chips before but, by Jaysuz, we got a tray of them and tucked in. I only had half a crown when I came to Dublin to play in an All-Ireland final. That's all I had and there were lads who hadn't even that! We ate the chips, went back to the hotel and went to bed. We got up next morning, went to mass and went on to Croke Park.'

Laois lost by a point after a second half that lasted forty-five minutes, during which Tipperary brought on nine substitutes. With teacher blood thick in his veins, Joe took the train home straight after the match so that he could finish his homework for the Christian Brothers in Portlaoise. 'We had a great big clock on the wall. I remember it was twenty-five to nine when I got home for dinner. My mother said, "You didn't win today?" – the hurling was on the radio or something – I said, "No." My father gave me a note for the Brothers in the morning.'

Joe is the only player to have been on the Laois minor team for five years in a row – 1933 to 1937. He continued to hurl until 1960 and says he got a welt from a hurl every time he went out. 'We didn't mind welts. We were working hard. That time we'd walk twenty mile and we'd work and walk home. People were much tougher. There was nothing to eat only bread and butter and the bacon that hung above you. We'd eat anything – carrots or turnips or cabbage.'

After he left school, Joe's father paid a welder to employ his son as an apprentice. Joe went without pay for the next three months – 'to see was I any good'. He got a salary of five shillings a week after that and 'got up to fifteen shillings by the time I finished'. His career path was set. 'I welded all my life – the whole life I'm welding.' He claims to have invented a crank shaft that cannot be broken – not even by a steam engine – but vows that he will take his secret to the grave. In the end, he had a business of his own outside Abbeyleix, lately sold to make way for a residential estate.

Micky is a quieter man, one of six children born into a farming family from Portlaoise. At seventy-eight, he has survived a bypass, a hernia and the complete loss of sight in his right eye. His gift for water-divining was revealed in his boyhood when his teacher, Joe's father, asked everyone to give it a try. Micky was the solitary success, although his anxious father insisted someone was 'codding' him. After school, he tried it again while checking on the cattle one evening and sure enough the magic sticks crackled over a source of water. 'I don't know is it a gift or not. It just works and that's all. I've seen hundreds of people who say they can do it but I've only met two or three who actually can.' Micky has four daughters and two sons but says none of them can divine. 'It just doesn't work that way.' When Micky married, he gave up farming and bought a machine for well-drilling. 'Every new house built around the country has to get water – and Micky is the man to find it,' asserts Joe.

JOHN MATHIS

Born c. 1927

Thatcher

Annagassan, County Louth

'I'm not sure when I was born,' says John Mathis. 'It was the wintertime.' We do our sums and work out that he is probably eighty-two years old. 'Aye, hey, 'bout that,' he concedes.

His is a strong dialect, characteristic of the older generation who live along the east coast of County Louth. He lives in a pink, thatched cottage that forms part of a labyrinth of cottages set up the Farm Road, a couple of miles southeast of Annagassan village. When his grandfather and father lived here, all of these buildings were thatched. Today, they are all slated or corrugated and the Mathis homestead is the odd one out.

That is as it should be for John Mathis is one of the last surviving old-style thatchers in the county. He was the fourth of seven children – two boys and five girls – schooled a mile south in Dillonstown. John left at the age of fourteen to make some shillings on the roads, building the drains of Drumcar, Martinstown and Salterstown. Sometimes, he helped his father and uncles with the thatching. The Mathis brothers were famous all over County Louth and thatched cottages from the Cooley Peninsula to Tallanstown.

John's father, Patrick, died following a stroke at the age of fifty-four. John, who was 'seventeen or eighteen' at the time, and his only brother quickly filled their father's boots.

John believes the basic techniques have changed little in a thousand years. 'It's all hand work,' he says. Though there are a few vital tools – he shows us a thatching fork, a veritable claw that you attach to your thumb for twisting and dragging the straw into locks. One of their first major jobs was at Seatown, the old de Courcy stronghold in Dundalk, known locally as 'Strawtown' because there were so many thatched roofs.

John says that the worst part of being a thatcher is that it can be 'a cold, old job', especially on the hands. Everyone wants their roofs thatched when the straw is fresh from the fields, and that is generally the tail end of autumn with the chill winds of winter already whistling in. In summertime, John was out repairing and patching up the roofs he had already built. 'I was never short of a job,' he says.

John never married. Today, his chief companion is a virulent and devoted sheepdog called Chester who lives on the settle bed and focuses a menacing growl on strangers until such time as they depart. There is also a cat who has not yet earned a name.

His principal living room is curiously oriental; dark furniture, the red glow of the Sacred Heart, a hint of burgundy lacquer rolling up from the white tiled fireplace. An elaborate mirror is framed on floral wallpaper. There are many photographs on the walls and on the tabletops. His parents, looking mildly surprised by the camera flash. Two of his sisters, one of whom died young. Another sister's grandson, grinning in his twenty-first-century school uniform. And here is young John himself, tall and lanky, cap on head, clambering up a ladder with an armful of reed straw and a purposeful frown.

When the weather is fair, you can see the Mountains of Mourne from John's house. The Irish Sea is directly to the north. The shore was home to an active fishing community until recent decades. 'I was never over the water,' says John. 'I was hardly in the water either, mind. I'm afraid of the sea.'

JOHNNY GOLDEN

Born 1937

Mechanic and Sexton

Dogarry, County Cavan

Johnny Golden never met his parents. He's not even sure who they were. 'But I know I was born in 1937,' he says, with a refreshing smile. By the time consciousness dawned on him, he was one of seventy young boys at the Sunbeam Home outside Bray, County Wicklow.

The Sunbeam was founded in 1874 by Lucinda Sullivan, one of those perpetually effective Victorian women who devoted their lives to improving the state of hospitals across Britain and Ireland. Entirely dependent upon voluntary support, its original purpose was to provide shelter for poor and homeless crippled children, whenever there were beds available. Many of its earliest inmates suffered from bone and joint disease, brought about by the consumption of 'tubercular milk of bovine origin'. It was still known as 'The Home for Crippled Children', or 'The Cripples' Home', until 1930, when it changed its name to the emphatically more optimistic Sunbeam Home.

In Johnny's day, the orphanage was supported by private donations, art sales, flower shows, musical concerts and the collection from St Patrick's Cathedral in Dublin, during the annual Boy Scouts and Girl Guides Service. Indeed, the Sunbeam had its own branch of scouts and one of Johnny's earliest memories was the summer of 1943 when 1,000 scouts from all over Ireland paraded in Lansdowne Road and Lord Somers presented the Sunbeam boys with a trophy.

Johnny speaks fondly of his days at the Sunbeam. Located on the Lower Dargle Road, the orphanage benefited from its proximity to the Dargle River and the Sugar Loaf mountain. Johnny climbed the mountain's quartzite slopes many times in his boyhood. From the summit, the boys would marvel that the snow-capped peaks of Wales could be so close. 'Ah, the Sunbeam was a great place,' Johnny says. He was lucky to make it through school alive. 'I used to walk in my sleep the odd time and I fell down the stairs. The way of it all was, I landed into the Adelaide Hospital but I was all right anyway.'

When Göring's Luftwaffe bombers struck Dublin in May 1941, the boys watched the explosions from their bedroom windows. During the Big Snow of 1947, they sleighed down the slopes of Bray Head on an old pram and made a giant snowman which they kept on building, higher and higher, thicker and thicker, so that Johnny swears 'it was still there in June or damned near it'. 'Ack, I was a just buck of a lad,' says he. 'I gave myself a cut on the knee making the sleigh and the cut is there yet.'

From the age of ten, he was educated at St Paul's National School in Bray. Three years later, the teenager said farewell to his Sunbeam colleagues and headed out into the world. The Sunbeam Home closed in 1960. 'I was back in Bray a couple of times since,' says Johnny, 'but it's a totally different place to what I knew.' He recently met one of his old school mates, by chance, when they both fetched up at the same bar counter in Killeshandra, County Cavan.

When Johnny left the Sunbeam, he and another boy, Richard Neale, were 'adopted' by a Miss Wilson who lived at Gulladoo just south of Carrigallen, County Leitrim. This was the age of the 'home boy' where orphans like Johnny were sent to work on farms in return for food and a bed, though the latter was often in the hayloft. In the morning, Johnny and Richard walked three miles barefoot to the local school in Arva where they 'learned damn all'. When school was over, they went to work digging potatoes, cutting turf and making hay. There was little or no pay for their work. When Miss Wilson died in 1963, 'the year Kennedy was shot', the Church of Ireland clergyman, Reverend Clements, transferred the boys to school at Corraspratten in County Cavan. It was quite a trek from Gulladoo and Johnny regularly 'landed in school when the roll call was over'. 'There was a good lot going to that school, forty or more,' says Johnny. 'They were farmers' children but a lot of those I knew are dead now.'

The boys continued to live in Miss Wilson's house until 1970, when they moved to Kilmore, County Cavan. Johnny later moved to Dogarry and was appointed sexton of the church in Killegar, ringing the bell, mowing between the graves and overseeing the general maintenance.

Johnny Golden. It sounds very rock and roll. The inspiration for the name may have been a Kerryman who led the Fenians in 1867 and was immortalised in 'The Ballad of Johnny Golden'. Johnny likes the name. He says Golden is a common family name in the Sligo–Leitrim area. 'I was supposed to have relations up this way,' he says.

He still speaks with a soft Wicklow accent and smokes a pipe with calm deliberation. He practices as a mechanic and electrician and is often identifiable by his grease-black overalls. He is a keen photographer, too, but can no longer find new film for his old Kodak camera. He travels on a bright red Honda 70 – maximum speed 50 mph – which he painted himself. He says it's a tradition that the Republic's Hondas are red while Northern Ireland's are blue. He wears slippers on his feet and a hat on his head but always rides bare-knuckled. On cold days, he wears a heavy woollen overcoat. 'Divil a dog, that's a curse of a coat,' he complains. 'The man who owned it before me is in the ground.' When not riding the bike, he is behind the wheel of a grey Ferguson TVO 20, built in 1952. Johnny is a vintage tractor enthusiast and frequently takes part in rallies and runs all across the country.

Johnny is a fine traditional musician and plays 'in the pubs the odd time'. He has mastered the piano, the button-key accordion, the tin whistle and 'the fiddle in any key'. He is also a well-known step-dancer. While we talk, he starts plucking on a toy ukulele and, before long, he has it tootling in a manner that compels every foot in the room to start tapping. A man in Cavan taught him piano. 'He'd make you play the same thing ten times. I got so used to it that one time I left the book to one side and started playing by note. I was fed up looking at the books.' He learned the other instruments 'by ear', he says. 'It is a very great gift to be able to play.'

LIAM O'SHEA

Born 1927

Blacksmith

Lauragh Forge, Killarney, County Kerry

Liam O'Shea is at work when we arrive, silhouetted in the horseshoe-shaped entrance of his forge. A tall, gallant man, he is dressed in blacksmith's apron and cap. His family have been farriers in Lauragh for at least six generations. The sound is ancient, as old as the Iron Age, with a merry lilt to its echo. The patient churning of the bellows. Dark smoky clouds hissing and rumbling over deep-red coals. The rhythm of the hammer, tongs and anvil as the red-hot metal bar is slowly beaten into the shape of a wheel-band.

The Lauragh Forge was built in the late eighteenth century to service the Marquis of Lansdowne's estate at nearby Derreen House. The landscape here is breathtakingly beautiful, all bubbling brooks, lush mosses and medieval trees. But no matter how spectacular the scenery might be, the Beara Peninsula was not an easy place to live when Liam's father, Mike O'Shea, was a young man in the 1890s. There was no employment, not much food and the families were simply too big for the cottages they lived in.

Born in 1875, Mike was the eldest of thirteen children, born and raised in a cottage by the forge. All of them went to America. Mike was the first to go when, in 1895, the twenty-year-old made his way to Queenstown (Cobh) and boarded a boat to New York. 'We don't know how he got the price to go,' says Liam's wife, Maureen. 'I suppose it must have been very little at the time. Then he sent home the fare for the next child to go. And that child did the same. That's how they all went out.'

By 1910, Mike was a well-established blacksmith in Manhattan, employing the skills his forbears had honed back in the Kerry forge where his son still works today. In later years, Mike would tell his family of winters so hard that a barrel of boiling water would freeze solid within an hour. 'Sometimes he held the nails in his mouth while shoeing,' says Liam. 'And with the heap of cold, it'd freeze onto his lip.'

In 1911, word arrived that Mike's mother had passed away. Mike's father was struggling to raise the younger children, including eight-year-old twins, so that same year, Mike sailed back to Ireland. Although he did briefly return to New York in 1920, perhaps to set up the twins, he succeeded to the Lauragh Forge on the death of his father in 1927 and never left Ireland again. Liam says that when asked of his time in America, his father would say that any day he spent in Kerry was better than the best day he had in New

York. None of Mike's siblings returned to Ireland, though one of his sisters, many years younger, flew over in 1982 to attend the wedding of Liam's oldest son.

Liam was born in 1927, the year his grandfather died. He was the fourth of six children, five of whom were alive for a family reunion in 2008. One brother became a garda in Tipperary, another settled in England and a third drove a bus in New York for close on thirty years.

Liam, the second son, was groomed for the Kerry forge from an early age. 'I stayed here with my father all the time,' he says. 'We were down here from the morning on and I tell you one thing, there was a lot of sweat lost in this forge.'

During the 1940s, Liam and his father worked side by side, straightening nails, moulding wheel-bands, shoeing donkeys and ponies and all the horses that were headed for the creamery. They were the only blacksmiths in the area, the closest options being Kenmare or Castletownbere. 'We worked all day and every day and sometimes Sunday too.' They made feeding troughs for sheep, grappling hooks for mussel farmers, field gates and fire-grates. 'And we were badly paid too,' says Liam. 'People just hadn't the money.'

'But we got all the gossip,' he laughs. 'If there was rain, you could fit six or seven in the forge … and because of the fire, you'd have plenty of callers. There were no cars in that time and everybody walked. My father had some kind of a gift of speech. He was in America and he had the gab. He would say something to everybody who passed on the road and they'd all stop. There's no stopping now. They're all in cars.'

Liam still regards his father with a degree of awe. 'I never asked him much because he wouldn't tell me,' he says. 'But I picked up a lot of information when he was giving it to other people that were in America with him and came back.' For instance, that the forge was once thatched and that Mike and his father had 'worked for the Lansdownes', but that it became 'hard to work for them' when things went 'soft' during the War of Independence.

Mike O'Shea died at the age of seventy-five in 1950, and Liam took the helm. On a good day, he would have seven horses shod by lunchtime. However, as the tractor began to replace the horse, Liam found he was obliged to pack his blacksmith's tools and set off around the Kingdom, often operating out of another man's forge in Kilgarvan.

Liam shows me a photo, dated 1909, of two old men standing outside his family forge with a donkey and cart. He leans forward and taps the photo gently with his forefinger. 'Them two men have no toothache now, hey?' he observes.

He's a witty, intelligent, charming man and loves gathering and redistributing information. He adores it when strangers arrive at the forge seeking directions because he almost certainly knows the answer. 'I knew every house between here and Castletownbere,' he claims, 'although, since the young crowd came in, I wouldn't know them all.'

In 1958, Liam married Maureen, a wee girl with a lilting voice from across the Healy Pass in Adrigole. Her voice is sometimes censorious but always musical and laced with humour. Liam has a bold streak but he is more than willing to be kept on the straight and narrow by his wife. Indeed, it is quite clear that this golden couple are still very much in love. When we suggest that Maureen stands in for a photograph,

she says no nine times in the same sentence. Liam gets her jacket, raises an eyebrow at her and slips her jacket on. No words are exchanged. He follows it up with an encouraging nod and out she comes for the snap.

The couple have three boys and a girl. Although very few horses came to be shod in the forge anymore, Liam taught his young sons all the tricks of the blacksmith's trade. However, proud as he is of them, it seems unlikely any will take on the forge. Liam is not without hope. 'If a fellow was young now and wanted to shoe horses, he could make plenty of money,' he reckons.

MARGARET 'NANA' McKENNY

Born 1918

Nurse and Nanny

Ardee, County Louth

As she enters her ninety-second year, Nana McKenny is entitled to sit back and exhale deeply. It has been a long, long time since she was born at the old farmhouse at Callystown by Clogherhead. The thatched farmstead, a fine, single-storey dwelling, with a loft, and a parlour and stables out the back, had been in her family for several generations. The house lay down a long wooded avenue and was surrounded by lush green fields in which her grandfather kept horses and cattle. 'There was only two fields between us and the sea,' says Nana, and many of her childhood days were spent on the beach. There was not much time for leisure though and, after school, Nana and her two brothers would return home to help on the farm, picking potatoes and cleaning turnips, though she refused to help with the dairy. 'I was afraid of cows,' she says. 'They were wicked looking with their crooked horns and I wouldn't touch them.'

Nana's four-year-old sister died in the early 1920s, 'choked by the croup' in the days before there was a cure. The event seems to have sparked a downward spiral in her father's life. An only son, he had by then inherited the Callystown farm. But he turned to drink with a vengeance and slowly but assuredly 'he drank the farm'. His children would not see him from dawn until dusk. When he finally stumbled home, he would take out his shotgun and start shooting up the night sky, shouting nonsense and obscenities. 'I could never talk to anyone about it,' says Nana quietly. 'It was so horrid. But we never knew him. We never really knew him as a father.'

Nana's mother tried to keep the farm going, employing another man to attend to the cattle. But as the debts mounted, the family were obliged to sell everything – the timber, the plough, the carts, the horses. Nana's most overpowering memory of this era is watching 'the little ass being taken away'. 'There was great heartbreak for us at that time.'

A brief respite came on Sundays, when the people of the parish gathered along Clogherhead pier for the weekly dance. The band would play on long after the sun's shadows had darkened the Mountains of Mourne to the north.

In 1938, Nana began an eight-year career as a nurse at St Bridget's Hospital on the Kells Road outside Ardee. She cycled to work from the farm every Monday morning, a twenty-six-kilometre (sixteen-mile)

155

journey, and stayed in the hospital for the next five nights, earning two pounds twenty-five pence a week. 'I didn't like it but I stayed in it,' she says. 'It was very hard work and we had to do night duty and all that, but we got a free uniform and free board and lodging.' Psychiatric help was still of a most rudimentary nature in 1940s Ireland. In the absence of tranquillisers, many of the more unruly patients were kept in cells. Alcohol, she observes, was to blame for ruining many of those she looked after. It was during this time that her father finally found peace when he passed away after a short battle with cancer. Nana's older brother, John, duly took on the farm and 'made a great job of restoring it'.

In 1946, Nana met and married her late husband, Paddy McKenny, then a young man following in his father's footsteps to become one of the best-known plumbers in County Louth. The following year, the newlyweds moved into the house on Ardee's Main Street where Nana lives today, just beside the old Wesleyan chapel. The street has changed a good deal over the ensuing sixty years. When Paddy and Nana moved in, most of the buildings were private houses with a few shops scattered in between. Today, Nana and her sister-in-law across the road are the only two residents left on a street dominated by commercial premises.

While Paddy earned a paltry two pounds a week, Nana focused on rearing their three children. She brought in some extra money by helping a local dressmaker. The couple worked hard and rarely holidayed. 'The farthest we travelled was Lough Derg,' she says. 'Myself and Paddy went on pilgrimage there twice.' Very occasionally, she visited Dublin – 'it was a great treat to get on the bus to Dublin for the day' – but she never really took to the city. She has never been to the west coast of Ireland or seen the Atlantic. 'Sure how would you do it?' she asks. 'We never had a car of our own and there were no tours at that time.'

Nana says that she 'hadn't a lot to smile about' in her life but it is clear from the photographs that abound throughout her house that the younger generations – her grandchildren, great-grandchildren and other children she has looked after – mean a great deal to her. Her son and his wife regularly call by to share a lunch with her and that 'keeps me in the chat and the craic'. Nana has wise counsel for anyone of senior vintage. 'You must make your bed in the morning, whatever you do. And you must never take to the chair or the bed. You have to keep on doing things.'

P.J. DAVIS

1924–2009

Car Mechanic and Steelworker

Ennistymon, County Clare

P.J. Davis was taught how to drive by his father, Paddy, in the early 1930s. The family had lived in Ennistymon, County Clare, for several generations. Paddy's father travelled the back roads of the Banner County, distributing coal and turf with a horse and cart. With the arrival of commercial motorisation in Ireland after the First World War, Paddy swapped the horse and cart for a one-ton lorry and became a full-time employee of the Griffin family, who owned the pub on Ennistymon's Bridge Street as well as a coal yard.

Eight of Paddy Davis's nine children emigrated to England, the exception was a son who still farms in Doolin. Some of his daughters became nurses in Stockport. One son joined the navy, another became a mechanic in Manchester.

Patrick Joseph 'P.J.' Davis, the fifth child, crossed the Irish Sea shortly before the outbreak of the Second World War. For the next fifteen years, he worked for the Rootes Group (now Chrysler) in Ryton-on-Dunsmore, near Coventry. The company's main business was the manufacture of Humber Hillman cars, one of the most popular brands of the 1930s and 1940s. P.J. worked in the foundry, making parts for Hillman's miscellaneous Hawks, Minx, Pullmans and Snipes ranges. 'I could tell you about every part of every car we made … where it came from, the engine, the cylinder, the pistons, the chassis, the valve, the whole lot.' General Montgomery drove about in one of their 4.1 litre Super Snipes, which he called 'Old Faithful'. In 1950, a Super Snipe that P.J. helped build took second place in the Monte Carlo Rally with Maurice Gatsonides and the Baron van Zuylen de Nyvelt behind the wheel.

During the early 1950s, P.J. returned to Ennistymon but there was insufficient work to keep him there. He returned to England and began work in the casting plant, blast furnace and rod mill of the Scunthorpe Steelworks in North Lincolnshire. Part of P.J.'s work involved spraying all the ballast dust out of the furnaces and transporting it to the railway company, which used the powder to buttress sleepers along the railway tracks. 'It'd give you powerful muscles,' he laughs.

In 1972, P.J. returned to Ennistymon once more but, this time, with a wife and several small children. He found work at the Stubben Saddles factory on the Lahinch Road, where he helped to maintain the

machines that enabled the saddlers to cut, bevel, sew, inlay, seam, quilt and pummel the leather. In his childhood, Ennistymon had half a dozen saddlers, but by the 1980s, Stubben's factory dominated the town. 'They were the dearest saddles money could buy,' says P.J. proudly.

P.J. says that Ennistymon has changed beyond recognition since the days of his youth. 'It used to be that every house was only one storey high,' he laughs. All the small pubs have either gone or been expanded into super-pubs. Your best chance for an old-world pint is at Nan Healy's. But, heeding his doctor's advice, P.J. doesn't drink anymore. Today, the widower keeps fit with a long, daily stroll through the streets of his hometown, irrespective of the weather. He also enjoys occasional visits from his five children who are all married and living in Ireland.

SONNY KINSELLA
& BART NOLAN

Born 1928 and 1929

Engineer and Docker

Dublin City

Sonny and Bart have been a double act for close on eighty years. They grew up in Dublin's inner-city Docklands in an age when the city, and the country at large, had turned its back on the once prosperous waterfront. Today, they amble around the Docklands like Statler and Waldorf from *The Muppet Show*, 'reporting' to the Queen B, aka Betty Ashe, who runs the St Andrew's Resource Centre, arguably the most socially proactive body on the southside. In between their ambling, Sonny is a learned local historian, while Bart has emerged as one of the key players in stamping out paedophilia in modern Ireland.

'We were both born on the one street, Townsend Street,' says Bart. 'I was at the City Quay end and he was from the snobby end.'

'He was always jealous of me,' interjects Sonny, 'because he came from the wild end.'

Sonny was educated in St Andrew's on Pearse Street, now the Resource Centre. Bart was schooled on City Quay. Bart assures Sonny that, while St Andrew's may have excelled itself during the 'Poet's Rebellion' of 1916, his school was known as 'Gloucester Street College'. 'College,' he repeats.

As a boy, Bart was up and out the door by six o'clock. He'd race down to the market and earn a few shillings delivering fruit and vegetables before school began. Waking up early wasn't difficult. Townsend Street wasn't exactly a quiet neighbourhood.

During the 1950s, there were approximately 22,500 families living in the parish of Westland Row. Most were crammed into the old Georgian tenement houses and run-down mews cottages on the back alleys. Conditions were emphatically substandard. In many cases, there was one tap and one toilet for four families. There were over a thousand people living on Townsend Street alone. Over forty people slept in Bart's house – he shared a room with his parents, two sisters and five brothers.

Sonny's case was even more extreme. He and his nine siblings lived in a ten-room house with fifty-four residents. 'It was very hard to get to sleep,' he says. 'But you got used to the noise.' One of his most persistent memories is of the hooves of the horses clattering along the cobblestones, with the wheels scratching behind them, as the mail coach trotted to meet the trains at Westland Row Station. And that was after the coalmen coughed and the babies woke and the mothers began shouting all over again.

The war years were exciting for children. When the first banana-boats came in, all the children raced down and caught bananas flying through the sky, thrown by the crew. Whenever a foreign navy ship came into port, the girls would gallop down to flirt and play. 'There'd be birds all over the place,' marvels Bart. The boys played football on the waterfront of Rogerson's Quay. Sometimes they wore gas masks when they played. 'They were a joke,' says Bart. 'There is no way they would have saved you.'

Before the First World War, Dublin's inner city had one of the highest mortality rates in Europe. Things weren't much better in the 1940s. 'You'd be going to a funeral every two days,' says Bart. Many of those who perished were young. 'We used to hear people saying, "Ah, but he was so old." But really, they'd only be forty-five. I'm eighty this year and that's old.' Sonny says there was a powerful sense of community. 'If you were in trouble, people helped you out.'

Bart left school at the age of fourteen and began delivering coal full time. He'd collect the coal from the merchants scattered between Butt Bridge and Sir John Rogerson's Quay and then drive his horse and cart up the river as far as Ussher's Quay and across the Liffey into Smithfield. 'The horse was vital,' he says. 'Everybody in the area had one. It was your security. If the horse didn't die, you wouldn't die.'

By 1945, Bart was working full time at the Dock Mill on Grand Canal Quay, waiting for the tugboats that hauled the grain ships into position. Otherwise, he queued up alongside all the other dockers and waited for the ganger's shout. 'But there wasn't much cargo coming in at that time,' he says. 'Maybe a bit of timber for Martin's. Or shifting some bananas.' His father worked as a docker at J.J. Carroll's and he had an uncle making galvanised baths in the Hammond Lane foundry, so they were both places to call by. In 1950, he moved to England, where he spent eleven years, primarily with Leyland Motors.

Meanwhile, Sonny was determined to climb a different ladder to his father, who worked for Dublin Corporation's Cleansing Department for fifty years, sweeping the streets with a brush, shovelling the muck into a handcart. 'Every day, he swept three or four long streets,' recalls Sonny. 'It made no odds if it was rain, hail or snow. He'd have a big heavy coal sack wrapped around his shoulders, with a nail through it to keep it in place, and a cap on his head.'

Sonny was born in 1928 and was named after Al Jolson's song 'Sonny Boy', the signature tune of that year's box office smash hit, *The Singing Fool*. His parents were both from Townsend Street. 'Everyone who lived in and around here integrated with one another,' he explains. 'You didn't really move out of the area. Everybody who lived in the street knew everybody else, so you had to meet someone!'

Sonny's first job was as a messenger boy for Eason's Bookshop on O'Connell Street. He subsequently worked for sixteen years at Harty Engineering in Ringsend and then at the CPC Foods factory on the Davitt Road. At the age of sixty-three, he seized a chance for early retirement so that he might concentrate on his writing and grandfatherly duties.

In 1993, Bart co-founded the campaign group Parents for Change, which has exposed several paedophiles in the Church and, more specifically, in Irish professional swimming. 'He's brought an awful lot to light that would have been forgotten only he never gave up the chase,' says Sonny proudly. 'The story needs to be told,' asserts Bart, citing Atticus Finch as his role model.

The Docklands today is an utterly different landscape to that of Sonny and Bart's childhood. Where once the boats unloaded their coal into the Gas Company hoppers, Martha Schwartz's swathes of red and green crisscross beneath the Daniel Libeskind-designed Grand Canal Theatre. Where once dead cats and coal sacks floated, barges now moor beneath cool hemispherical railings and giant towers that light up at night. Today, these two old dockers walk the street and point out the places where the coal yards and foundries once stood. They know all the old names. 'We used to call that row of houses Lourdes,' says Bart. 'You had to have something wrong with you to get a house in it, but then you always seemed to get the miracle cure the instant you were in.'

'It's strange to see it all now,' says Sonny. 'There's a bit of sadness for us. Docklands is gone. We lost our jobs and now we lost our heritage. But people are better off of course. And this is a great neighbourhood to live in. We're probably just a bit jealous of the new Docklanders.'

TERESA McGERTY

Born 1925

Shopkeeper and Publican

Longfield, County Cavan

Teresa Galligan, the youngest of eight, was born in the townland of Derrinlester, County Cavan, where her father Thomas ran a fifty-acre farm. Educated in Killygorman, she left school to work as a shopkeeper in Celbridge, County Kildare, and, later, in Lurgan, County Armagh.

In 1952, the twenty-seven-year-old left the Galligan homestead, crossed the border into County Leitrim and married local farmer Jack McGerty. Jack's aunt, Roseanne Kiernan, had died two years earlier, leaving him a two-storey pub and a small farm at the quiet crossroads of Longfield.

Teresa's shopkeeping experience stood her in good stead to run the pub. She and Jack modernised the interior, unrolled linoleum on the floor, installed a new bar counter and built shelves up every wall. Teresa remembers the days as being busy. 'But if you want to make ends meet, you have to make an effort of yourself.'

As well as being a publican, Jack was widely known as a rate collector, auctioneer and cattle dealer. He was up at the crack of dawn to check on his own herd. Teresa opened the grocery at eight thirty every morning, when the nearby creamery opened for business. Paraffin was the big seller in the early years, before electricity came. 'And a lot of people had chatty-bangers,' she says, referring to the battery-operated lamps they sold.

As mother of Michael and John, she was forever washing, ironing and cooking, while simultaneously maintaining polite banter with customers behind the bar. The McGertys never holidayed; someone had to look after the cattle. However, Teresa occasionally escaped on the barefoot, three-day pilgrimage to St Patrick's Purgatory on Lough Derg. She grimaces at the memory of the unappetising 'Lough Derg Soup' (hot water, salt and pepper) that pilgrims drink during the first twenty-four-hour fast. Like a surprising number of Ireland's landladies, Teresa is a lifelong Pioneer. Her only taste was a sip of champagne in celebration of the birth of neighbour and old friend Lord Kilbracken's youngest son, Seán, but she found it sweet and uninteresting.

For half a century, the McGertys' unassuming grocery bar was amongst the most popular rural retreats in County Leitrim, famed for its impromptu dance nights and music sessions. Performers included the flamboyant Cork-born banjo player Margaret Barry, Paddy Moloney of The Chieftains and the acclaimed uillean piper Leo Rowsome.

During their first year, the McGertys also benefited from the infamous bona fide rule. Under the terms of the 1872 Licensing Act, if a man 'travelled in good faith' for a distance of at least three miles by public thoroughfare from the place he spent the previous night, then he was entitled to be served after midnight and on Sundays (Sunday drinking was then otherwise outlawed). Longfield is five miles from Killeshandra and five miles from Carrigallen, so the pub was understandably popular with those eager to capitalise on the 1872 Act. Teresa habitually concocted tea and sandwiches to sober up such late-night revellers and Jack often drove them home. The bona fide law was abolished in 1953.

When Jack died in March 1999, Teresa and her son, John, closed up the pub. The bar counter and shelves were removed and the space where so many people laughed and danced became their living room. Where once the walls were stacked with whiskey, firelighters, Weetabix and turpentine, today there are just a few poignant photographs, including one of the McGerty's grocery bar in happy days gone by.

WILLIE DAVEY

Born 1940

Labourer

Ballinvoher, Ballymote, County Sligo

'Did you not read all about me in the papers?' he asks, his face breaking into a broad George Clooney grin. 'Ah, now, my story is a long one. I'd need some time to track the memory back.'

We are standing in Willie's roadside prefab in Ballinvoher, a couple of miles outside Ballymote. The shed was brought here by a truck earlier in the month. This is Willie's new home. 'It's big enough for one man,' he says, leaning against the Ranger cooker that heats his water and radiators. Just beside us is the 'one acre' cottage, in near ruinous condition, where Willie was born seventy years ago. It is the last survivor from a cluster of houses built a hundred years ago and originally belonged to Willie's grandfather, Tom Davey. Willie looks at it with mild discomfort. 'It'd take some money to fix now,' he says.

There are many who believe that Irish civilisation began in County Sligo. Certainly when you stand high up on the cave-studded slopes of Keshcorran Hill, there is an otherworldly sensation that mankind was here a thousand generations ago. This is the parish where Tom Davey was born and reared. 'And a great man he was,' says Willie. Tom operated a brick lime-kiln at the foot of the hill, burning the rocks into lime as white as snow and then selling the powder on to local farmers.

When not making lime, Tom often played his fiddle, particularly 'at dances in the houses at them times'. The Daveys were a musical family and Willie's father was a fine flautist. 'We could all sing a bit, ballads and things, big band stuff, but not the pop music.' At that moment, a cuckoo shoots out from a clock on the kitchen wall and lets out twelve whoops to celebrate midday. 'He's come on at a bad time,' observes Willie drolly.

During the 1920s, Willie's father Tommy went to work as a builder in New York. He later moved to Manchester, where he met and married a Galway girl who had been living in England for thirteen years. The couple returned to Sligo just before the outbreak of the Second World War and Tommy got a job with Sligo County Council. A big man, he spent too much of his earnings on alcohol. 'He wasn't used to drink because he hadn't got the cash,' says Willie. 'He wasn't too bad on it but it would change him and he was better without it.'

Willie was the third youngest of the couple's eleven children, all raised in that small, corrugated cottage.

'There was a lot of us in it,' he mutters quietly. Several of his siblings are now dead. One brother lives nearby. Another is in England. He has one sister 'married down in Cork' and another who's a nun on a mission somewhere deep in the African interior.

Like thousands of other Irish children, Willie Davey walked to school barefoot every day. 'Your feet get hard on frosty roads quick enough,' he says. School was a three-mile walk away at Drumcormick, near Lough Arrow. The children sat at long wooden desks, fifteen per desk, and counted down the minutes before they could go home. If you left your lunch in the desk too long, a rat would get at it and many was the lunchtime that Willie and his pals spent whacking rats with sticks. 'Sometimes, we might not have any lunch at all, only a bit of bread, and when you come back home you wouldn't have a lot more. But that's the sort of times we had.'

'I can tell you,' he goes on, 'there was nothing to eat one time. People who were poor had nothing at all. There was a lot of big families and how they got on, I do not know. There were too many children. They had no jobs half the time. There was no work, no money, no food. You might work two or three days a week but there was no such thing as dole or an allowance. There was too many people and we were all working by hand, cutting on the bog and putting down crops, because if you didn't work, you'd go hungry. There was no choice. It was slavery.'

In his twenties, Willie went to England. 'Sure you had to go somewhere,' he says. 'I went all around looking for work – I'm not the only man who will tell you that story – but I hadn't much luck.'

By the mid-1960s, he was building up a reputation as the feistiest hell-raiser in Ballymote – he maintains there wasn't much to do except go to the pub 'and there were twenty-four pubs at that time'. His chosen tipple was a lethal cocktail of Irish whiskey and red wine. 'I wouldn't hold it too well and I'd just let myself go,' he says, shaking his head. 'I used to demolish houses, you know, breaking down doors and things. I was a wild man.' While we talk, I notice that his T-shirt sports an image of the cops from the spoof *Reno 911!* with the tagline 'Don't Let the Badge Fool Ya'. Willie was constantly in trouble with the law. He spent many nights in the local gaol, but when he drove a Honda 50 through the window of the Ballymote Garda Station, he was sent to prison in Dublin. 'Oh, yes,' he grins, 'I've been down the rocky road to Dublin and I've sung the song many times.'

'I had to calm down,' he says. 'I was getting old and there was always something that the law would be after me for.' He was also struggling to be served. 'There was many who wouldn't give Willie Davey a drink,' he says. 'They were doing it for my own good but I don't know if they would let me in now either.' Willie quit drinking in 1990 but, nearly twenty years later, allows himself the occasional glass of wine at funerals and Christmas.

Willie feels somewhat estranged from modern society. It's all 'so different now' that 'people have other ways of enjoying themselves, with televisions and telephones and DVDs'. Ballymote is a 'very different town now – different shops, different people'. The younger generations seem incapable of understanding how bad things were. 'They won't listen and they'd nearly be asking you, "What is a bog?" now.'

Willie's gruff, short sentences disguise the humour that makes his eyebrows dance, his lips twitch and his chin jut. He holds his smile for a generous length of time. He does not relish the idea of living alone in his new home. 'I was a ladies man,' he says, 'but I never met the right lady to marry.'

FRANK O'BRIEN

Born 1922

Publican

Emily Square, Athy, County Kildare

'I could tell you the history of most of the old families in this town,' says Frank. It comes with the territory, of course, being a third generation publican. But Frank didn't just meet people in his family's pub. His father operated a sideline business as a fuel distributor during the 1930s and young Frank was his principal haulier. 'I used to bring twelve hundredweight of coals down from the Wolf Hill Collieries and deliver it all around. That's how I got to know every house.'

As we talk, customers of every vintage amble into the grocery bar. They come to buy Bovril and Barry's tea, birthday cards and creamy soups, detergents, Kimberly Mikados, and a few slices of corn beef. Every one of them says 'Hello Frank' as they reach the front of the green and white counter. And Frank rounds off the ensuing banter with a peaceful, 'Go raibh maith agat.'

Frank has been working at O'Brien's since he was old enough to nod. During the 1930s, the pub was a popular haunt for First World War veterans. 'They'd get their pension and have a couple of pints and reminisce,' recalls Frank. 'You'd hear the same stories every week. Poor fellows. It all came back to them. They'd been prisoners of war and were badly shell-shocked. The things they'd seen. There were men who'd lost arms and legs and everything. It's like that song, 'Johnny, I Hardly Knew Ye' … that was written for soldiers from Athy who were killed out in Sri Lanka.'

In 1940, Frank's father contracted rheumatic fever and the eighteen-year-old was obliged to take the helm. The pub had been in the family since 1875, when Frank's grandfather, Stephen O'Brien, bought it from James Leahy, a prominent GAA patron and Home Rule MP for South Kildare. Stephen was born in County Kilkenny in 1830 but moved to Dublin during the Great Famine and opened up a tea-house on Dorset Street. When his doctor advised him to return to the countryside for the good of his health, Stephen settled upon the thriving market town of Athy and bought the pub. 'And there's been no change in here since then,' says Frank.

Stephen's wife, Annie, was a sea captain's daughter from Drogheda, who bore him eleven children. Frank remembers her well. 'Queen Victoria, we called her. You had to be all cleaned up with your hair brushed and buttons done up before you were brought into her presence.'

All of Stephen O'Brien's children stayed in Ireland but Patrick, the eldest, died as a baby. Another son, George, an excise officer in Dundalk, succumbed to the Spanish flu of 1919, leaving a large family. Most of the remainder lived into their nineties, including Frank's father – also Frank – the sixth child. 'When Daddy got sick, I asked the doctor what his chances were,' says Frank. 'He said, "If I get him to Thursday, he'll live." Well, he wasn't able for the stairs after, but he lived to be ninety-one and he was alert until the day he died.'

In 1921, Frank O'Brien Senior married Annie Kelly from the nearby village of Ballitore. Frank, the eldest of four, was born the following year. His mother also had publican blood in her veins, dating back to 1812 when Edward Kelly, her great-grandfather, leased a pub in Ballitore. Frank remembers seeing the ledgers of Kelly's pub in his youth. One entry that particularly struck a chord concerned the dispatch of two creels of barley to Cassidy's Distillery in Monasterevin in 1846 with a note that the potato crop appeared to be afflicted with the same disease as the previous year.

In 1932, the year Granny Annie died, de Valera's new government hosted the Eucharistic Congress in Dublin. Frank recalls how, during that week, his father was raising funds to buy a loudspeaker to install in the park in Athy so they 'could broadcast the Eucharistic ceremony for people who couldn't go to Dublin'. He chanced upon Captain Hosie, a popular war veteran who ran the main foundry in Athy, one of the few places offering full-time employment during those lean years. Captain Hosie duly astonished Athy when he ordered an enormous wireless from Siemens and installed it in the park. 'Nobody had ever heard anything like it,' says Frank. 'Radio was such a novelty! We had a wireless at home but this was the very best that could be got. And there was never as many in the park since or before.'

Today, the walls of O'Brien's pub are festooned with sporting memorabilia – photographs of the victorious Ryder Cup team, calendars full of Kildare footballers, posters of grinning rugby players. On my last visit, several customers had both eyes firmly fixed on the horses galloping on an overhead television screen. Frank was a keen sportsman in his younger years and hurled for Athy when they won Kildare's junior championship final in 1945. To stay fit, he played a lot of badminton and table tennis. 'We played table tennis all over Leinster,' says Frank. 'In Church of Ireland halls and parochial halls and everywhere. It was big time. There was no class distinction, no religious distinction. And there was always someone looking for a match.'

Frank says the evolution of the affordable car in the 1950s marked the end of that particular sporting era. 'Before the cars came, we went everywhere by bicycles. But the very minute the motor car came in, that was it, end of story. Everybody went off on their own and it finished off the whole damned thing.'

One of the greatest gatherings of bicycles in Athy during this age was when Carlow's footballers took on Dublin for the Leinster final in 1944. 'There were thousands of bicycles on the square,' says Frank. 'Not hundreds but thousands. And ponies and traps everywhere.' It was deemed the match of the decade when Carlow won by a goal to gain their only Leinster title to date. 'The Carlow Fifteen was an outstanding team,' concludes Frank.

Frank believes the 1940s were one of the most interesting decades in Ireland. That's not simply because he was one of the first people to see the desolation of North Strand after the Germans bombed Dublin in 1941. In his mind, the summer of 1946 was a defining moment. That was the year when thousands of

Dubliners, mostly civil servants and office workers, made their way into the countryside in order to help save the harvest. 'It was incredible to see so many people from so many different backgrounds coming together to help,' he says.

In 1952, Frank met and married Tríona Carney of Kiltimagh, County Mayo, his wife of fifty-seven years. For their honeymoon, they drove a black Ford over the Cork and Kerry mountains and up the west coast. In due course, they had a son, also Frank, who lives in Detroit, and a daughter, Judith, who married an American and now helps run the pub.

'We're still doing what we always did,' says Frank who is, ironically, a lifelong Pioneer. 'But it's getting harder. Being a publican is a full-time job and weekends are big for business. I need to be here the whole eight days, Monday and all.'

REST IN PEACE

Atty Dowling 1916–2005

Bill Burgess 1902–2007

Bob Murphy 1909–2002

Christy Kelly 1933–2008

Donal Duffy 1920–2007

Festus Nee 1934–2008

George Thomas 1926–2009

Jack MacNamara 1923–2005

John Murphy 1925–2006

Jack O'Neill 1925–2008

John Shannon 1922–2005

Michael 'Patsy' Flanagan 1924–2009

Michael King 1925–2006

Mick Lawlor 1927–2004

Nellie Kelly 1922–2007

Paddy Canny 1919–2008

P.J. Davis 1924–2009

Pat Gleeson 1913–2006

Pat 'Rua' Reilly 1907–2008

Tom Connolly 1917–2008

ACKNOWLEDGEMENTS

Many individuals have provided generous support and welcome encouragement to the ever-evolving 'Vanishing Ireland' project. Evidently the changing face of Irish society is a matter of much interest to people all over the world.

We would like to thank the team at Hachette for all their help, particularly Ciara Doorley who orchestrated the creation of these pages, and Karen Carty from Anú Design, who looked after the design so capably.

We would also like to extend our gratitude to the following for miscellaneous assistance along the way.

Johnny and Chloe Alexander • Cullen Allen • Anto Ardee • Betty Ashe • Daria Blackwell • Peter Blake • Peter and Chacha Bland • Jo Blennerhassett • Alice Boyle • Eugene and Roseanne Brady • James Brady • Dermot Brennan • Michael Brennan • Brooklane Hotel, Kenmare • Andrew and Nicola Bunbury • William and Emily Bunbury • Tom Butler • Carlow Rootsweb • Redmond Cabot • Liz and Andy Cairns • Pat Carter • Nan Clarke (who so eloquently recited Wordsworth's 'Daffodils') • Mikey Coneally • John Cooke • Tim Coote • Colm Costello • Quentin and Ger Cooper • Angus Craigie • Jim and Anita Crothers • Peter and Maura Crowley • Michael Cryan • Danny Cullen • Ruth Cunney • Andrew and Siobhan Davidson • Brian and Sally Davidson • Esther de Barra • Leon C. de Barra • Doireann de Buitlear • Angela Delaney • Paddy Donoghue • Tom Donovan • Ruth Doran • Tom Dowling • Lesley Fennell • June Finnegan • Pauline Flood • Gilly and Larry Fogg • Alice and Matthew Forde • Allen Foster • Ed and Alex Galvin • The Knight and Countess of Glin • Sean Godley • Sophie Gorman • Tim Goulding • Adam and Justin Green • Linda Hand • Ann Healy (Nenagh Daycare Centre) • Hillview Nursing Home, Carlow • Jonathan Irwin • Hugo Jellett • Arthur Johnson • Fred Johnson • Ally Jones • Gráinne Kavanagh • Morgan and Sara Kavanagh • Jed and Lucy Kelly • Martin Kelly • Mary Kelly • Dave Kennedy • Sue Kilbracken • Piers and Harriet Landseer • Maeve Liffey • Fred Madden • Susan Macken • Johnny and Lucy Madden • Peter Mantel • Sheila McCabe • Pat McDonagh • Helen McInerney • Niamh McNamara • Nicholas McNicholas • Sean McQuillan • John Mescal • Niamh Molloy (and her exceedingly good coffee) • Gavin Moore • Miriam Moore • Dominic Moran • Catherine Muldoon • Vinny Murphy • Gus Nichols • Isabella Rose Nolan • Oisin and Aoife Nolan • Judith O'Brien • Mark Onions • John Onions • Lochlann and Vicky O'Mearain • Father Ian O'Neill • Denis O'Reilly (Wild Wicklow Tours) • Jo Patton • Serena Perceval • Archie Phelan • Pat and Yvonne Phelan • Michael Purcell • Michael Quinlan • Alex Raben • Charlie and Michaela Raben • Ben and Jessica Rathdonnell • Michael O'Shea • Sheila Reilly • Jack Rogers • Ron Rosenstock • Jessica Slingsby • Rowan Somerville • Sully • John Swiney • Lauren Swiney • Tom and Sasha Sykes • Fiona Symes • Orla of Vaughan's Pub • Conor Walsh • Sean and Shiela Walsh • Trish Walsh • Lorraine Ward • Mary White, TD • Catherine Whitehead • Marcus and Olga Williams • Nick and Becky Wilkinson • Liam Dowling • Seamus Dowling • Peter Ward • The Hillview Nursing Home (Carlow)